DESIGN FOR SHOPPING

DESIGN FOR SHOPPING

NEW RETAIL INTERIORS
SARA MANUELLI

Laurence King Publishing

Published in 2006 by
Laurence King Publishing Ltd
71 Great Russell Street
London WC1B 3BP
T: +44 20 7430 8850
F: +44 20 7430 8880
E: enquiries@laurenceking.co.uk
www.laurenceking.co.uk

A catalogue record for this book is available from the British Library.

ISBN-13: 978-1-85669-450-6
ISBN-10: 1-85669-450-X

Printed in China

Project managed by Lara Maiklem
Designed by John Round Design

CONTENTS

INTRODUCTION

THE WAY WE SHOP TODAY

The market has traditionally been the place for the exchange of goods and has defined the relationship between the retailer and the consumer. Mass culture and globalization resulted in the evolution of the marketplace into a wondrous array of subtle formats. Today, the digital technology revolution and the impact of saturated markets have altered it even further. What was once the marketplace has now evolved into a zone of experience and lifestyle, and shopping has changed with it. The basic behavioural patterns of consumer activity have now taken on a social and cultural complexity. Commodity has become increasingly substituted or incorporated into services; retail is gradually morphing into leisure; and art has been installed to elevate the purchasing act – as if by purifying the shopping experience, one could forget the very principles of commodity and the capital it is based upon.

As the culture of consumerism has advanced, the complexity of consumer thinking has been analyzed and revealed. It is clear that prominent in the psychology of the consumer are desire, longing and daydreaming. Sociologist and author Colin Campbell noted that people have a self-indulgence to desire, which he coined 'modern autonomous imaginative hedonism' (*Romantic Ethic and the Spirit of Modern Consumerism*, 1987). Paul Ginsborg, author and historian, also writes that 'The visible practice of consumption becomes just a small part of a complex model of individual hedonism, most of which takes place in the imagination of the consumer' (*Berlusconi, Television, Power and Patrimony*, 2004). The retail machine supports this theory by continuing to form a pathway for the shopper to this world of consumer hedonism. We can see in the sales of the Apple iPod, Nokia N-Gage, Nintendo Gameboy and the Sony PSP that personal immersion is a consumable aspect of dreaming and imagination.

In this immersive world, brand alone is no longer the single inducement. Retailers have progressed to the creation of complex environments that can provoke an emotional response from their customers. The post-shopping age has created a whole set of challenges for retailers and designers. Epicenters, guerilla retailing, brand architecture and sensory environments are just of some of the new buzzwords being used. Brands like Bulgari, Gucci and Salvatore Ferragamo have expanded their retail businesses into branded hotels and bars. The distinction between buying and living is becoming strategically indistinguishable. These days, good-looking retail space is no longer enough. The post-shopping consumer expects to be engaged and entertained. The drive to create an unforgettable shopping experience, conducted in an amazing environment, has to be tempered by the need to pace the shopper and is underpinned by improving the customer's experience and service.

Retailers, architects and designers are constantly looking for ways of maximizing retail space. Fashion seems particularly drawn to the visual clout that architects can bring – the creative constructions of architects can add longevity and respectability to the otherwise ephemeral world of fashion. In the 1980s, Esprit owner, Doug Tompkins, commissioned Norman Foster, Ettore Sottsass, and Shiro Kuramata to design several stores. Rei Kawakubo, founder of Comme des Garçons, soon followed in 1983 with a New York store designed with Takao Kawasaki and a series of commissions with Future Systems). In 1986 came John Pawson's minimalist temple for Calvin Klein, in the 1990s Giorgio Armani's worldwide stores designed by Claudio

1 Bulgari Hotel, Milan.

2 Café Gucci, Milan

3 The Continentale, one of five Ferragamo-owned hotels in Florence.

1

2

3

Silvestrin, and the Noughties saw the Prada Epicenters by Rem Koolhaas and Herzog & de Meuron.

Some British grocers have also – albeit more rarely – sought architectural assistance. In the UK, for example, the 1988 Sainsbury's store in London's Camden Town, by Nicholas Grimshaw and Partners, and the 1999 'environmentally responsible' Greenwich branch of Sainsbury's, by Paul Hinkin of Chetwood Associates. Elsewhere in Europe the Austrian, family-run supermarket chain, MPreis, has 120 stores, dotted around the country. Over the past 15 years commissions for these have been given to up-and-coming architects. Before this relatively recent vogue for architecturally designed stores, however, other great architects had also ventured into retail design. At the end of the nineteenth century, Louis H Sullivan designed the Carson Pirie Scott and Company building in Chicago, Carlo Scarpa created the Venice Olivetti showroom in 1958 and in 1964 Hans Hollein designed the Retti Candles Shop in Vienna – this is to name but a few.

Yet even a high-profile architect cannot always supply the necessary transformation for a company's retail ambitions. In February 2004, Marks & Spencer opened its first Lifestore in Gateshead, Newcastle, UK, dedicated to selling the company's homeware range of products. In March 2003, Marks & Spencer lured Vittorio Radice from the London-based department store Selfridges to be the executive director of the new Marks & Spencer Home business. While at Selfridges he had established a notion of 'shopping as theatre' and had masterminded the store's expansion, first to Manchester and then to Birmingham in the landmark Future Systems building (pages 78–81) that turned the brand into a powerful shopping destination.

At Marks & Spencer, Radice repeated the process by commissioning John Pawson to design and build a full-size house inside the Gateshead location. The different rooms inside the house – styled by head of in-store visual merchandising Ilse Crawford – conveyed the new Marks & Spencer direction. At the back of the house, a dramatic staircase rose through a double height space to three rooms above. However, six months later, a board reshuffle, a change of management style and lucklustre sales resulted in the closure of Lifestore, and all future plans to open further stores were cancelled.

NEW APPROACHES

For top-end fashion labels, retail kudos is measured in buildings, megastores and epicenters. Luxury goods are now sold in modern cathedrals to consumerism – spaces that move large amounts of capital, selling famous label garments and even larger amounts of accessories. From the display of technology in the Prada epicenters (pages 38–43), to the commissioning of high-profile architects and the use of art installations, all of these are devices that aim to elevate the act of purchase into something resembling a ritual. More and more retail environments are appropriating terms and experience models of leisure places like spas, hotels, museums. It is not enough to just install a café; a store must now become a retreat, an escape, and also a destination.

There is a curatorial approach to the selection of merchandise, evident in concept stores like Colette in Paris, Corso Como in Milan and Dover Street Market in London (pages 174–177). Furniture showrooms, home furnishing stores, even top end grocery formats like the Sainsbury's

4 Esprit, London, by Foster and Partners.

5 Comme des Garçons, New York, by Future Systems.

6 Calvin Klein, New York, by John Pawson.

7 Giorgio Armani, Hong Kong, by Claudio Silvestrin.

4

5

6

7

8

9

Market in London, instil a value that promises a better, stylish and more healthy lifestyle. Some, like fashion designer Giorgio Armani, have taken the 'holistic vision' idea even further and used shopping as way to develop property sites in rundown areas of the city. In Milan, Italy, Armani acquired a Nestlé factory and commissioned architect Tadao Ando to transform the whole area (near Porta Genova) into a fashion space, theatre and gallery centre. Similarly, in Shanghai, China, he has opened a multi-concept store of 1,100 square metres (11,840 square feet), designed by Claudio Silvestrin, Doriana and Massimiliano Fuksas.

In a contrasting approach to building shopping empires, a consumer backlash has manifested itself most vehemently in the anti-globalization demonstrations of the early Noughties. At a micro level, consumer patterns, arguably influenced by a 'No Logo' approach, are changing. Freegan, Dumpster Diving, Recycle This! Food not Bombs are just some of the groups that have sprung up in favour of recycling, low consumption levels and freedom from brand domination. These groups often subsist as marginal counter cultures that abstain from buying and spending and contrast traditional shopping with alternative forms of consumption. Freegans, for example, obtain their food from supermarket refuse bins – often still packaged and in fresh condition – while Dumpster Diving practitioners delight in recycling objects from the bins of luxury apartment blocks.

In retail, the term 'guerrilla architecture' is being increasingly borrowed to denote a low-cost, provisional space arranged for shopping. In design terms it manifests itself as a more transient, light, portable, industrial chic approach, as opposed to the permanent, sleek detailing of the 'white box' of the 1980s and 1990s. Brands like Camper

(pages 100–101), Levi's, Comme des Garçons and Umbro are all employing these tactics as a marketing tool to sell more clothes and as a way out of long and expensive leases and high-cost buildings. Paradoxically, the first official spate of 'guerrilla stores' came from Comme des Garçons, the brand that first promoted the marriage between retail and high profile architects. However, guerilla architecture has very little reference to the anti-establishment antics of architectural groups involved in urban interventions, art installations and public art. As journalist Elaine Knutt wrote in the architectural magazine *Icon* (issue 020), 'It's hard to imagine anyone breaking the law for the sake of selling a Kangol hat or Comme des Garçons perfume: for these brands guerrilla retailing is more about finding an alternative channel for communicating with customers… Guerrilla retailing isn't so much a retail revolution, as a turn of the fashion wheel.'

NEW SCENARIOS

Unsurprisingly, it is in cities such as Berlin and Tokyo that we find some of the most interesting examples of contemporary retail design. Berlin, after a period spent as a giant construction site, is now gathering momentum as a city with unlimited potential, even though it lacks a prominent city centre and many parts of the city are still being rediscovered. Rents and property prices are low, making Berlin one of the cheaper European cities to live and generate business in. The mood here is very much 'self-made' with a younger generation of architects, designers and independent retailers taking control of disused spaces for innovative store concepts. The attitude that formed much of the city's nightlife in the early 1990s,

8 Armani Headquarters and Theatre, Milan, by Tadao Ando.

9 Carson, Pirie, Scott & Co., Chicago, by Louis H. Sullivan.

10

11

12

when clubs with a limited life span would spring up in warehouses, is now extending to retail. Comme des Garçons' first guerrilla store was in Berlin, because it arguably drew inspiration from the inhabitants' anti-monetary approach to retail. Concepts like BLESS (pages 102–105) and smart-travelling store (pages 154–157) are both valid examples of how low budget can breed creativity.

At the opposite end of the spectrum lies Tokyo with its conspicuous consumption and Western brand fetishes. Areas like Omotesando Avenue are where luxury names rush to open gleaming 'boutique palazzos' – usually high-rise buildings designed by renowned architects. The Dior building by SANAA, Tod's building by Toyo Ito and Prada's epicenter by Herzog & de Meuron, are not only valid examples of commercial architecture, but also reveal an increased tendency towards focusing on the façade of the building, in same cases leaving the interiors to shop fitters and designers. In a city of such building density and high property prices, a stunning 'outside' is often more powerful in terms of brand awareness than a very expensive advertising campaign.

'The "boutique palazzo" syndrome does run rampant through our profession, the thinking being that the façade is urban, the street the stage and the brand leveraged by the sophistication and expense that goes into the public "face" of the retail design,' says Hani Rashid of American architecture firm Asymptote. 'But while on streets like Madison Avenue, Via Monte Napoleone and Rodeo Drive that strategy is all-important, the strategy for newer, establishing brands might very well be the opposite. The interior experience is what makes the brand memorable and establishes it as sophisticated, fresh and fashionable,

and it is here that architects need to pay much closer attention to the actual experience as opposed to the image.'

TAILORING FOR DIFFERENT MIND-SETS

As free location becomes scarce and rents rise, retailers are pushed into finding other ways of picking customers with new format strategies, locations and services. 'You need to tailor your offer to location as well as to different mind-sets,' says Rune Gustafson, senior partner at brand strategy and design group Lippincott Mercer. 'You might well have the same demographic profiles, but customers' needs change constantly. So you segment the customers by attitude and develop both different products and different retail formats.'

According to Gustafson, with people constantly pressed for time it is not only important to satisfy certain needs fairly quickly, but also to be able to tap in the 'share of purse', *i.e.* the need for different purchases at different moments. The UK-based, high-street chain-store chemist Boots, for example, has opened in London's Holborn area a store that can fulfil the high traffic flow of the area. In this particular store, basket sizes are smaller and the emphasis is on toiletries and health and beauty brands for the local office workers. As supermarkets are taking an increasing proportion of consumer's spending, they are keen to tap into other markets beyond groceries. They are bidding for the housewife's household budget, money left over from the weekly shop to invest in, for example, some clothes. 'People make trade-offs in budgets,' says Gustafson, 'and retailers are keen to have a piece of the pie.'

The installation of in-store technology should ideally be fitted because of need, rather than just the desire for high-tech gimmicks. In 2002, Sainsbury's opened a pilot

10 Olivetti showroom, Venice, by Carlo Scarpa.

11 Marks & Spencer Lifestore, Gateshead, UK, by John Pawson.

12 Colette, Paris.

store for time-pressured families in Hazel Grove near Stockport, UK. The store was driven by technology-enabling services and worked closely with the retail design group 20/20 on customer focus groups. The 'bottoms up' approach delivered a 3,700 square metre (39,830 square foot) store with a number of discrete areas, each including elements of new technology. A vending machine stocking 150 products, including milk and bread, proved popular among night-shift workers. A trial 'Pocket shopper' device was also installed that used a key fob to scan the bar codes on products so that they could then be used to print a shopping list, either to use in-store or to upload onto a computer to order online from home. Three interactive displays for children, devised in partnership with the Science Museum in London, were visited by over 23,000 people in the first 12 weeks of opening and proved to be a very successful marriage between technology, retail and play.

The boundaries between retail and leisure 'mind-sets' are also creating interesting concepts. After becoming firmly established in department stores, cafés are now springing up in bookstores. Brands like Starbucks are installing CD burners in their coffee bars and even publishing their own music CDs, in a bid to establish a 'theme'.

'With the advent of brands like H&M, Zara and Mango we have witnessed a formidable process of democratization of fashion,' adds Gustafson. Here, store formats and shop-fitting elements are kept simple and flexible, while the emphasis is on procuring the customer a 'fast fashion fix' with an average of 16 collections per year. Buying cheaper items is considered 'smart', even for those who can afford expensive clothing, and there is a tangible shift from luxury stores to more bargain-priced discount chains.

From railway stations to airports and petrol forecourts, travel locations are ripe with retail potential. 'Because people spend a huge amount of time in airports and stations, it is important that retailers manage this time in a reassuring way,' says Gustafson. The Sainsbury's branch in London's Paddington Station, for example, has a TV screen inside with the trains' departures times. For designers and architects these are challenging new places. 'I am fascinated with the hyper-shopping spaces in airports such as Copenhagen, Heathrow, Singapore and Schiphol. These spaces are in desperate need of some truly inspired retail designs, and we hold out hope to get a chance to try our hand at these part urban, part-mall, part-theatre, and part-duty-free heaven and part-transit hell environments!' says Rashid.

ARE YOU BEING SERVED?

Service is becoming one of the most important elements defining the shopping experience. As the world of commerce is increasingly revolutionized by a trend of dematerialization, there is a move away from the market economy, with its emphasis on physical goods, possessions and ownership, into a new era dominated by service, supply and access. 'In retail, it's the move away from buying and selling mass-produced, manufactured goods into a new understanding that supply is more valuable than that which is being supplied. It's a world of lifestyle and brand identification. A world that treasures customer relations and guards, jealously, the mediation between the consumers and the provider. It's a topsy-turvy world. Sometimes goods are given away for free and profits made from support rather than through mere one-off transactions,' says Neil Churcher, associate professor at the Interaction Design Institute, Ivrea, Italy.

13 Sainsbury's Market at Terence Conran's Bluebird gastrodome, London.

14 The reconstruction of Berlin has resulted in the generation of many innovative store concepts.

15 Epicenter Prada, Tokyo, by Herzog & de Meuron.

13

14

15

Often called the 'service economy', or the 'access economy', its commercial value is often framed within time rather than by physicality. 'A service can only be supplied and judged as it is experienced and that happens in real time. In retail it's the decision to enter a store, or when taking in the atmosphere, identifying with what is on offer or being provided for at the counter. Those intangible moments cannot be possessed like a product, but have weight and impact on retail sales,' says Churcher.

But what are the implications for designers? 'In the way that services are experiences, the creation of services themselves can only be realized by designing the experience itself. It is not enough to specialize in 2D and 3D, products or graphics, or in physical concepts like point of sale or brand image. The designer of services needs to think in time and be able to craft the experience of the consumer, as they themselves would experience it. Service creation is, in many ways, the ultimate design process for the consumer society, because the act of consumption itself is (like service) an experience cycle,' adds Churcher.

Apple is the ultimate example of this shift in retail. Previously only known for the Apple Macintosh computer, a product that was sold and revised into new versions every year, Apple is now a lifestyle choice that is encapsulated by a singular design style that touches everything Apple. Apple is a cool outlet (pages 126–129) of all things Apple. It is a revolutionary way of listening to your music collection and it is a radical change. 'Even Apple's most "product"-like thing, the iPod, is an elusive wrap of style, immersive lifestyle and service,' says Churcher. 'Apple is more lifestyle choice than product sale and that streams right through its outlets. Apple Store is a way for the company to regain the ground

lost by its traditional franchise method of product supply (which always had a reputation for sluggishness). More importantly, Apple wanted to control its identity on the high street. Whether it's hardware, mediated services, software or accessories, the message is the same; the lifestyle is singular. It's a club.'

TECHNOLOGY HAS MADE THE CUSTOMER KING

New technology, 'the digital information revolution', has impacted hugely on the way the world shops. Online access has meant that demand has become increasingly more sophisticated. Defined by some as simply the era of the consumer, the shift in power has swayed towards the customer. 'Yet the technologies that have made this happen are altering aspects of all relationships in the retail chain, from the behavior of the consumer, the means of retail supply, promotions of goods, even the concept of the goods themselves. These alterations are by-products of a much larger technological impact on the market economy,' says Churcher.

Mediation is one altering factor, *i.e.* ways to form closer communications and relationships 'in between' the retail supplier and the customer. 'Any supplier not exploiting this "mediated" space may find the gap filled by techno-opportunists who exploit the space to build their own relationships with consumers as a way of controlling customer desire. Online access to knowledge is a way of controlling the market,' says Churcher. As journalist Paul Markillie points out in the *Economist*'s survey of consumer power (8 April, 2005), '80 percent of Ford's customers in the USA have already researched their purchase on the web before they arrive at a showroom, and most come with a

16 Sainsbury's high-tech pilot store at Hazel Grove, Stockport, UK.

17 Starbucks, South Molton Street, London.

18 H&M store, Germany.

16

17

18

19

20

specification sheet of the precise car from the dealer's stock'. At the other end of the spending power spectrum, many teenagers now find the idea of actually purchasing a DVD or CD somewhat alien. They have grown up in an era of easy access and network download. For them, the cost of the packaging and the medium, as well as the additional retail costs, seem unwarranted, especially as buying a CD or DVD represents the slowest way to get hold of the goods.

For retailers and designers this calls for a new conceptualization of retail space. In the near future retailers are not looking to create places just to sell, but to suggest, evoke and promise the essence of the brand. Volkswagen's impressive Autostadt opened in June 2000 as a 25-hectare (62-acre) 'theme park for cars' at its Wolfsburg, Germany headquarters. The 48-metre (158-foot) -high tower can hold up to 800 new cars, ready for delivery. Autostadt is the architectural embodiment of a move away from conventional showrooms towards an inviting and interactive retail space.

GLOBAL VERSUS LOCAL

In an increasingly globalized world, we like to think of retail as an enterprise that can be easily and successfully exported. But how can retailers translate offers and concepts to other countries and cultures? Brand awareness, advertising and the media have made European shoppers, for example, very similar to each other. The brands on sale in the high street are often the same and, one would assume, so are the shopping patterns. Yet within this process of creeping standardization there are other differences, such as regional variety, different demographics and economic cycles. In consequence, retailers need to cater for an increasingly 'international', yet 'local' customer.

The incredible expansion of Tesco, the UK-based supermarket chain, into Eastern Europe and most recently its entry into the massive Chinese market, makes it one of the largest world retailers, together with the French company Carrefour and US-based Wal-Mart. In retail terms, Tesco could be seen as a successful example of an 'adaptor': a retailer that owns stores in its own country but has also managed to adapt the concept to the regional needs of other countries. By tailoring the offer to local eating habits, the shop has managed to strike a balance between indigenous ranges and universal brands. Food retailer Carrefour is also seen as a positive example of the 'adaptor' model, especially in China, where it is competing in the country's booming retail market. While its sale of snakes and turtles might seem bizarre to a Western customer, it is merely a response to the dietary and cultural requirements of that region.

The success of stores such as B&Q in China, there called 'Bai An Ju', also proves the winning adaptor formula. The UK-based DIY store has entered the country in a time of property development, growth in home ownership and government liberalization of the housing market. These factors, coupled with a rising interest among the Chinese population in home decoration, have ensured the expansion and commercial success of the chain. In addition, retail adaptors see foreign markets as a chance to expand their horizons, perhaps with new store formats. 'In China, shoppers are suddenly given a choice they had never had or seen before,' says Gustafson in 'Crossing Continents', his article in the 2003 summer publication of *Lens* from UK strategy and design consultancy 20/20. 'When Carrefour and B&Q entered China, they went for the latest technology, the

19 Zara store, Oxford Street, London.

20 Tesco supermarket, Lodz, Poland.

21

22

newest store concepts, the most advanced retail offer. So even if they entered a market which is not as developed, consumers quickly got used to a much higher choice and retail offer.'

An alternative retail model, often quoted for international expansion, is the 'repeater', comprising of a simple format and a back-of-house system. This model has been taken up by brands such as the Gap, Starbucks, McDonald's and the Body Shop. Of course there is no such thing as a true 'repeater', and even brands like McDonald's cater to the country's culinary tastes with minor variations. The success of repeaters is that they are cheap to replicate and can expand quickly, although they can also become saturated and seem 'old-hat'. On the other hand, although adaptors might take more market research to set up, once the offer is defined it is perfectly integrated with the consumer's demands and needs. An understanding of the language and cultural patterns of behaviour, price, product qualities and positioning are all crucial elements to consider in global expansion.

This book intends to address some of the current themes in retail design. In 'Glorious Old Brands' it looks at how the revitalization of existing brands happens via retail design. Within the process of reinvention and promotion a flagship store often maintains a stronger impact than a well-orchestrated advertising campaign. 'Technology and Shopping' addresses issues of how technology is being used within retail design – for efficiency, for example, point of sales systems, customer databases, inventory databases, RFID (Radio Frequency Identification) technology, and also as a way of communicating how innovative, forward-thinking and up-to-date a particular brand is. 'Fashionable

Stopovers' questions the issue of whether visiting a shop is similar to visiting a museum or a church and whether the status of the destination can eclipse the merchandise in it. In 'Play and Shopping' the book looks at how irony, play and a slight sense of subversion can be brought in to revitalize the shopping experience – ideas, rather than costly shop fittings, is the theme underlying the collection of case studies.

'New Ways and Places to Shop' looks at how brands, such as telecoms and computers, are favouring the 'service' and the 'lifestyle' model over the sale of goods. It also looks at how brand architecture is being employed to capture the essence of a brand. The lifestyle experience charts the rise of the lifestyle model in retail through food, interiors, jewellery end even eyewear. It shows how retail works at creating an aspirational mode of living as a tool for selling. Finally, 'Fashion and Art' examines how shops have taken to incorporating art and commissioning artists to create a more 'elevated' and entertaining environment. As art curator Germano Celant remarked on the occasion of Prada's presentation of its new Epicenters, 'In the end, it all fits together: art, fashion, architecture, design – even shopping. It's all theatre, really: a modern spectacle for a modern world.'

21 McDonald's restaurant, Germany.

22 Volkswagen Autostadt, Wolfsburg, Germany.

Pringle, in London's New Bond Street, projects an image of modern British glamour while at the same time referencing the company's traditional Scottish roots.

INTRODUCTION

In recent years there has been a spate of established and conventional brands being given a new lease of life through strategic reinvention. This has been achieved through methods such as re-branding and repositioning of the brand values through advertising campaigns and revamping product lines. In particular, the quintessentially British labels Burberry, Aquascutum, Mulberry, Aspreys, Dunhill and Pringle have all been busy reinventing their image by drawing on the qualitative values of their heritage and by replacing outdated values with a sleeker, more contemporary format. Crucial to this ethos has been the flagship store, a synthesis of a glorious old brand's values.

So common has this brand re-evaluation process been, that today it is often referred to by the design press as 'doing a Burberry'. When CEO Rosemary Bravo took over the reins of the company in 1990, Burberry revamped its image through the hiring of new designers and the launch of successful spin-offs, such as the Burberry bikini. New ads, depicting 'Cool Britannia' faces Kate Moss and Stella Tennant, helped the raincoat brand become hip again. In 2004 alone, Burberry opened stores in Houston (Texas, USA), Tokyo (Japan), Americana Manhasset (outside New York, USA), Charlotte (North Carolina, USA), King of Prussia (Pennsylvania, USA), Scottsdale (Arizona, USA), Boca Raton (Florida, USA), Burjuman Centre (Dubai), Rome (Italy), São Paulo (Brazil) and enlarged and refurbished its stores in San Francisco (USA) and Paris (France). Its retail architecture roll-out fittingly reflected the healthy financial status of the company.

Similarly, the British brand Mulberry benefited financially in 2001 from the sale of 41 percent of the business to Club 21,the Singaporean fashion and hotel group owned by husband and wife team Ben Seng and Christina Ong, who also run Armani in the UK. £2.6m was invested in a makeover that was geared to repositioning Mulberry and aimed at expanding its customer base with a complete kit of creative strategic ideas as well as creating several new retail sites.

In March 2002 Pringle of Scotland approached Wells Mackereth to come up with a retail design concept to suit a major repositioning for the luxury fashion brand. London-based Wells Mackereth, comprising Sally Mackereth and James Wells, have a history of working extensively in both retail and leisure. Their other projects include the restaurant Smiths of Smithfield, the restaurant and hotel West Street Bar, Korres Natural Products store, Yoga Studios and Stone Island/CP Company.

INTERVIEW WITH SALLY MACKERETH OF WELLS MACKERETH, LONDON, UK

Wells Mackereth was commissioned to create Pringle's first flagship store in London. What was the brief?

'We were commissioned by Pringle to help them turn shopping into an intriguing and tactile experience. The programme of building involved a store for Heathrow Airport in London, one in Tokyo, a flagship store in New Bond Street, London, a store in Sloane Street, London (with showrooms and company HQ). Other stores were planned for New York and Milan and the production of a design manual for concessions for use by licensees around the world.'

What elements of its heritage and new positioning did you employ as inspiration for the design.

'Pringle has a very strong brand history. It was founded in 1815 as a knitwear company in Scotland and has a royal warrant. You could summarize it as "cabbies and kings" (*i.e.* for taxi drivers and royalty alike). But over the years it lost its identity and developed an extremely different range of clothing. It had no dedicated store, so it was decided to reinvigorate the company by moving it on from the dull, golf-sweater image to a cooler, covetable brand. The brief to Wells Mackereth was to turn the flagship into the brand. A site was found on New Bond Street in London, where Armani had a store previously. The challenge was how to seduce people in such a highly charged shopping environment as New Bond Street. There is an element of theatre about the contemporary shopping experience. You have to create a certain thrill.'

How did your retail design help to regenerate the brand?

'With a brand like Pringle it was essential to establish a kind of narrative that translated through the details. The shop was pivotal in Pringle's "new" message, yet the brand had to be cautious in order not to alienate the customers. Just before opening the New Bond Street store, Wells Mackereth was informed of the need to anticipate Pringle's new retail concept with a space at Heathrow Airport's Terminal 3 and in Tokyo, Japan. We found ourselves, therefore, in the odd position of developing a concept manual before the flagship had actually opened.'

Wells Mackereth has worked both in retail and leisure environments. Are the two fields becoming increasingly connected?

'You need to activate the seduction process through a little piece of theatre; the creation of a certain thrill can really only be achieved in three dimensions. You may check "netaporter.com" for fashion's latest arrivals, but you still want to enjoy the physicality of a shop's space. Going shopping is the new "going to church". Pawson's Calvin Klein store is immaculately detailed – it's a cathedral to retail. The fact that some Trappist monks, who had seen images of the store, decided to hire Pawson to design their monastery and robes merely reinforces the idea of a certain type of ascetic architecture that can be applied to both mundane and spiritual places.'

What is the main difference between architects and retail designers?

'Architects know how to create a place instead of a space. They are generally in a better position than retail designers to understand the scale, the pace and the longevity of a space. As architects we can create narratives, which help explain ideas to clients and get people excited. Architecture as a discipline brings into play all the different elements, like the gallery element, the hotel and the entertainment.'

If the building becomes the message, and the flagship becomes the brand, is architecture more potent in its communication than, say, an advertising campaign?

'Flagships need to be seen as a reinforcement of the brand. There needs to be a suitability of the shopping experience to what the brand is trying to do. They are really two different ways. With retail design, you have to work within budgets and consider issues like the rent. With advertising it's difficult to quantify; you can't really say if a double-page spread in *Vogue* has paid for itself. It's really about the power of two dimensions versus the power of three dimensions.'

1

Legendary fashion label Gucci was given a sleek and sexy turnaround by fashion designer Tom Ford when he joined the company in 1990. Before Ford, Gucci had slipped from a 1960s iconic fashion brand into a company ruined by family feuds and with a somewhat relaxed attitude towards licensing. Ford set about successfully reinventing Gucci as the ultimate modern luxury house, every star's favourite and first choice for galas and catwalk struts.

Gucci's two-decade-old Fifth Avenue store reopened its doors in 2000 after a lavish 15-month renovation by architect William Sofield (this after the dramatic 72-month renovation of the whole company under Tom Ford). Studio Sofield's portfolio ranges from landscape design to residential, retail, hospitality and corporate office design.

With 3,252 square metres (35,000 square feet) of space and several floors of corporate offices, Gucci is counting on the beginning of a comeback for the Fifth Avenue shopping district. Banking on its heritage, the New York store aims to be 'a Modernist reinterpretation of Gucci's long-standing, signature marble-and-wood environments, introduced in the 1960s'. Standing at the corner of 54th Street, the new concrete-and-

1 Interlocking display units, within the open floor plan, define the space sculpturally.

2 Banking on its heritage, the New York Gucci store aims to be a Modernist reinterpretation of Gucci's long-standing signature marble-and-wood environments that were introduced in the 1960s.

2

3

4

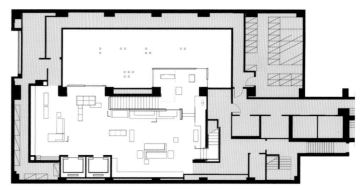

Second floor

limestone embodiment of Gucci Inc., marks the midpoint between the Avenue's two major players: Bergdorf Goodman and Saks Fifth Avenue.

Decked out in rosewood, travertine and stainless steel, the new design is modern throughout and luxurious. The open floor plan is punctuated by interlocking display units that define spaces sculpturally while allowing for dynamic seasonal change. Reflective surfaces, pale lacquers, rich but quiet finishes and generous six-metre (18.5-foot) ceilings on the ground floor complement the horizontal lines of the cantilevered salons, while carefully hand-crafted Modernist fixtures add to a cinematic but subtle interior. Light is treated as a material. A complex combination of HID (High Intensity Discharge), metal halide, incandescent, halogen and fluorescent illumination washes the interiors with a veil of light that complements the sensual, tactile qualities of the store and the sumptuous clothing within it.

With its five floors (increased from three), two elevators, maze of stairways, and umpteen balconies that look out onto other floors, the store is a celebration of luxury consumption and status symbols. The cabinets and finishes are in a seven-layer, hand-rubbed lacquer and the single, central fitting salons are fully upholstered in hand-tufted New Zealand mohair, off of which are the private fitting chambers complete with customer-controlled 'day-to-night' adjustable lighting. An additional private salon and fitting room is located on the fourth floor. Custom-designed and crafted vitrines and cabinets appear to float in space on transparent Lucite bases, providing plateaus of display and luminosity.

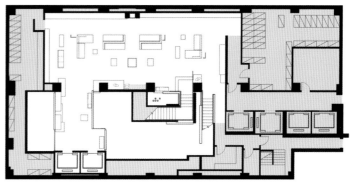

Third floor

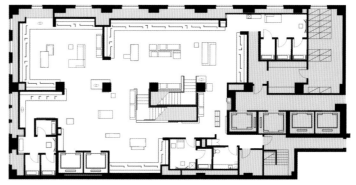

Fourth floor

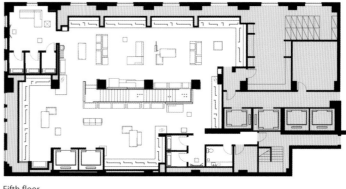

Fifth floor
5

3 Reflective surfaces, pale lacquers and generous six-metre (18.5-foot) ceilings on the ground floor complement the horizontal lines of the cantilevered salons above.

4 Decked out in rosewood, travertine and stainless steel, the design is at the same time both modern and luxurious.

5 Second-, third-, fourth- and fifth-floor plans show the open-plan style of the store with the main circulation staircase at the centre.

For years, the Liberty mock-Tudor building has been a favourite among those in search of the quintessential British shopping experience. The building dates back to 1924 and, although full of heritage, its quaint layout was struggling to keep up with the more theatrical experience offered by nearby London department stores such as Selfridges. In a bid to inject some much-needed contemporary glamour, the London-based design group 20/20 was approached to revitalize the 3,716-square-metre (40,000-square-foot) store overlooking Regent Street.

'The starting point involved a precise definition of what the brand represented, and using this insight to remain faithful to the Liberty brand in all areas of the store design. This resulted in an experience description of an "aesthetic emporium", reflecting the design-centred ethos of the store's founder, Arthur Lasenby Liberty,' says Simon Stacey, then team leader at 20/20 and now a partner at Lippincott Mercer.

A pulsing 'Liberty purple' light installation draws customers to the new entrance. Inside, all three floors have been opened up with windows revealing the store to Regent Street and a new escalator providing greater visibility across the floors and movement between them, again using purple light to create movement and intrigue.

Each floor features a defining 'signature statement' – a distinctive element of product presentation, merchandising or service that creates Liberty's point of difference. On the ground floor, the dramatic-looking cosmetics hall is centred on large, dark-wood 'play tables', where women can indulge in testing their favourite beauty products. The idea of allowing the customers to try out the products creates a warm and relaxed atmosphere. Above them, hang commissioned sculptures – abstracted from Liberty flower prints and using crystal glass, once again in the Liberty purple. Coloured Plexiglas towers, with the signage information inspired by Charles Eames' 'House of Cards', direct customers up to the first floor and the women's shoes and lingerie department.

1

2

3

LIBERTY Regent House

1
Regent House

Link with Tudor House

WC

Women's Shoes
& Lingerie

G
Regent House

Exit to Regent Street

Cosmetics
& Fragrance
Skincare

LG
Regent House

Link with Tudor House

WC

Menswear
& Accessories
Men's Shoes
Arthur's bar/restaurant

1 Specially commissioned sculptures using crystal glass are abstracted from Liberty flower prints and hang from the ceiling in the cosmetics hall.

2 Each floor of Liberty is defined by a distinctive element of product presentation that creates the unique Liberty point of difference.

3 On the ground floor, the dramatic-looking cosmetic hall enables women to test and touch their favourite products.

5

6

Here, the signature statements are sculptural plinths, which function as display systems for the shoes, allowing them to take centre stage. The contemporary feel of the plinths is contrasted with antique Venetian glass mirrors and Liberty fabric sculptures, commissioned from textile design graduates.

On the lower ground floor, in the menswear, shirts and accessories department, the atmosphere turns to that of a men's club. A 35-metre (115-foot), red Chinese-lacquered shirt and tie 'bar' allows customers to browse for product by colour and fabric. The oriental theme draws on one of Arthur Lasenby Liberty's early inspirations, and is updated for the forms and proportions of the shoe and luggage department, again in red Chinese-lacquer. The café, appropriately named 'Arthur's', is a more obvious testament to the founder. Here, customers can relax surrounded by ever-changing exhibitions of art, photography and sculpture.

'Liberty Regent House translates the richness and colour of the brand's heritage, with a contemporary aesthetic that now gives customers a new, exciting and unique experience of the Liberty brand,' says Stacey.

4 The shirt and tie counter in the menswear department allows customers to browse by colour and fabric.

5 The newly installed escalator provides greater visibility across the three floors, all of which are bathed in the trademark Liberty purple light.

6 The Chinese red lacquer that is used for the menswear department intends to convey a clubby, decadent feel.

Mulberry was set up in Somerset, England, in the 1970s by Roger Saul, using a family gift of £500 and with his mother, Joan, as a partner. Originally a belt designer, Saul developed a collection of leather accessories from which grew a brand that has since become synonymous with high-quality luxury products ranging from men's and women's clothing and accessories to stationery and home furnishings. By 1992, the annual turnover was £50 million, and on its 25th anniversary, in 1996, Mulberry floated on the AIM market. However, the late 1990s version of luxury failed to be satisfied by a brand like Mulberry, which started to falter. In 2000, 41 percent of the business was sold to Club 21, the Singaporean fashion and hotel group run by husband and wife team Ben Seng and Christina Ong, who also run Armani in the UK.

Design group FOUR IV was appointed by Mulberry to reposition the British brand as a major player in the luxury market. FOUR IV implemented a research strategy geared to find out where Mulberry sat in the landscape of luxury brands. The findings expressed the brand as 'English', 'inspirational' and 'aspirational'. This became the essential communicating elements of the brand, through product, stores, concessions, graphics and other communications. The new Mulberry brand identity, created by FOUR IV, retained the distinctive Mulberry tree logo, redrawn to bring it in line with the new modern luxury values of the company. The tree was also used as a stand-alone logo, particularly on signature leather products, and a new contemporary typeface began to be used in corporate applications.

The New Bond Street store intends to represent Mulberry's heritage as an English, witty brand that specializes in exquisite leathers and detailing. The new store exudes this character – from the leather-panelled staircase to the oak furniture. The re-evaluated brand's newly focused and coherent ranges of leather accessories, contemporary

1

1 The new Mulberry flagship store on New Bond Street embodies the brand's position in the luxury market.

2 A leather-panelled staircase leads to the menswear department on the lower ground floor. The leather-clad back wall contains semi-hidden doors that lead into the changing rooms.

2

3 Suede walled changing rooms and low lighting create a sense of boudoir-style lavishness.

3

4

4 Leather mannequins and bespoke lighting attempt to challenge the division that has traditionally existed between shop fittings and art.

5

clothing and homeware are given individualized areas. Menswear is situated on the lower ground floor and has a leather-clad back wall, containing secret panels leading into changing rooms reminiscent of a stately home. The patterns of the landscaped formal gardens at the Mulberry factory in Shepton Mallet are picked out on the rug. A long table – a piece for the new Mulberry – is oak inset with leather, and amber glass doorknobs, made in Cornwall, complete the look and feel.

British crafted structures focus on the essence and techniques employed by Mulberry. In various departments, bespoke leather mannequins, chandeliers and other ephemera aim to challenge the traditional division between shop fitting and art. Bronze and timber rails hang on leather straps; these clothes-horse-type frames carry

gentlemen's trousers. On the ground floor, in leather accessories, luggage and homeware each occupy their own environment, with elements such as chocolate limestone flooring helping to set the various scenes. A leather-panelled staircase leads to womenswear, past a conservatory and bespoke, porcelain chandeliers. Moving into the great hall a huge bevelled mirror reflects the length of two of the signature long tables, and suede-walled changing rooms create boudoir lavishness.

6

5 Bronze and timber are employed throughout the shop for display units.

6 On the ground floor, luggage and home wear is artfully arranged to enact various scenes.

Pringle of Scotland was founded in 1815 by Robert Pringle, a young entrepreneur who recognized the business potential of providing fine-quality, knitted underwear to the well-to-do people of Scotland. Pringle was also one of the first companies to produce machine-knitted garments that could be worn as outerwear, and to coin the term 'knitwear'. In the 1950s, Pringle became famous among Hollywood starlets such as Audrey Hepburn for its figure-hugging twinsets. At the beginning of the Noughties, the fashion label went through a revamp campaign that emphasized the brand's heritage while also injecting a slight edge. From Madonna to Robbie Williams, the quintessential diamond pattern was, as a result, once again present in the wardrobes of the famous.

Pringle's heritage involves fine materials (wool, cashmere and silk) and excellent craftsmanship. With the advertising strapline, 'Be materialistic', the new store in New Bond Street aimed to celebrate the love of materials and to play out the drama between textures – soft against hard, matt against shiny. The design of the space reinforces a subliminal message of the brand's historical Scottish roots through scale, colour, material and reference, while at the same time projecting a bold, new international image of 'British glamour'. The contrasts are embodied by materials such as concrete set against leather detailing by Bill Amberg.

1

2

1 Large tables, covered in felt, are reminiscent of billiard tables and function as useful display units.

2 Hard materials like concrete and stone play against the 'softer' elements, such as the luxurious leather detailing by Bill Amberg.

3

The architects, Wells Mackereth, introduced a narrative by juxtaposing images within the two-floor environment. They wanted to create a sense of a story, and to do so they used images, objects that act as references or beacons of an atmosphere. Details and materials such as the silk damask wall, the stone fireplace and the sweeping staircase make subliminal reference to the scale and decadence of a Scottish castle. Slabs of stone, containing fossils, and rich, dark hide transport visitors from the fumes of London to the wild, open Scottish Highlands. To emphasize this, there is a reference to outdoor artist Andy Goldsworthy's work taming nature, as well as to artist Anish Kapoor's sense of scale. A visit to Robert Pringle's library in his home in Scotland inspired the more 'domestic' approach to the various departments. The menswear department, upstairs, has a long plinth with a decanter, bar stools and two large tables covered in felt and leather, reminiscent of billiard tables. A small circular room, designed like the turret of a castle, contains the

childrenswear collection. Mackereth chose a rich, deep purple colour as a backdrop for the pastel-hued clothing. Like the collection itself, it was important that aspects of the store were quite playful, such as the clear resin antlers that are mounted in the turret-style winding stairwell.

A second store in Sloane Street was designed to suit a more relaxed, Chelsea spirit. Mixing materials and textures, Wells Mackereth created a distinctly Pringle atmosphere by bringing elements of the great outdoors (Pringle Golf) and London living together within the façade of a grand Victorian townhouse. While the New Bond Street store was conceived as the 'Big House', the Sloane street outlet is viewed as more of a weekend place – a bit younger and more relaxed.

3 The sweeping staircase leads into the menswear department, which is designed to evoke the intimacy of a domestic environment.

4 From left: ground- and first-floor plans, with the curved staircase at the bottom right.

5 The stone fireplace is a direct reference to a Scottish castle, while the clear resin antlers mounted above it inject a dose of humour. The deep purple seating and a rich, dark cowhide on the floor represent the luxurious element.

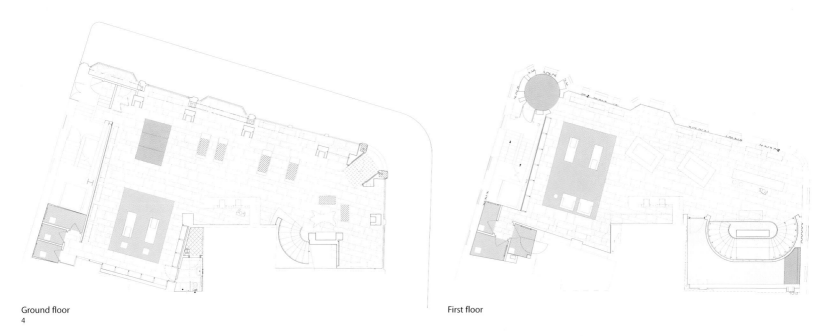

Ground floor
4

First floor

5

Set on Rodeo Drive, the LA Prada store is the media-savvy result of a collaboration between a high-profile architect, Rem Koolhaas, and a major fashion brand. It contains a mix of free space and areas where the structure is exposed.

TECHNOLOGY AND SHOPPING

INTRODUCTION

Technology has increasingly become a defining element of the shopping experience. With pioneering vision, the Prada Epicenters, commissioned in 2002 in the USA, kick-started an endless discussion about the role that technology has in retail – whether it is about entertainment and/or aiding the act of consumption. While heading the research and concept team at the Office for Metropolitan Architecture (OMA), Markus Schaefer worked closely with architect Rem Koolhaas, Reed Kram from Reed Kram Media Design in Stockholm, Sweden, IDEO and the Prada team on the brand's environment, image and communication.

In 2003, Schaefer joined with Hiromi Hosoya to set up Hosoya Schaefer Architects, a Zurich-based practice that divides its time between creating concepts for clients in field as diverse as politics, university management, integrated regional planning, retail and corporate identity. According to Hosoya Schaefer Architects, digital technologies that provide an alternative to spatial continuity, along with branding and media that affect representation, have fundamentally changed the way we understand and use space. Markus Schaefer talks of the experience of conceiving technology for a retail environment.

INTERVIEW WITH MARKUS SCHAEFER OF HOSOYA SCHAEFER ARCHITECTS, ZURICH, SWITZERLAND

Why is technology used in shopping?

'First, it is used for the efficiency it allows. Point of sale systems, customer databases and inventory databases are tools that were generated strictly for the logistical side of the business. Now, many of these systems are created in order to be seen, and sometimes even used, by clients. In this sense, technology simply is part of how shops are currently organized and run. Second, shopping, especially when it is shopping for fashion and trends, is still associated with newness, and technology is a very important signifier of the new. Shops use technology to show that they are up-to-date. Often the communication that is achieved with displays or projections could also be achieved with print or other media, but that would be seen as old-fashioned. The medium is very much the message in a shopping environment.

When Rem Koolhaas began the collaboration with Miuccia Prada and Patrizio Bertelli several years ago, they were interested in something different, a totally new approach to retailing. With a team of fellow students studying with Koolhaas at Harvard University, we had just completed work on the *Harvard Guide to Shopping*, where we analyzed how shopping had invaded all other activities in the city. The citizen had become a consumer in the museum shop as much as in the university merchandising shop, and in areas as diverse as the airport and the church. We also looked at the relentless drive for newness and its modernizing and innovative, yet often frivolous, force. We were interested in using these insights to respond to the classical questions of architecture – use, the role of the collective, representation and space. Technology integrated into space allowed for interactions that were architectural rather than menu-driven. The system was to allow us, next to increasing efficiency and providing a better service, to represent the company and its cultural context in new ways. We were interested in juxtaposing to the hermetic logic of branded space, information and images that were raw, rough, strange, taken from the public domain or taken from the company and presented without the need to turn them into a seamless story. I believe that companies exist in a spectrum between identity and innovation. Identity, a branded image, is dependent on stability and control; innovation is based on accepting the unexpected. We hoped to use technology to do the latter rather than only the former.'

How do architecture and interaction design relate? How can interaction design bring the whole technological vision together within a retail environment?

'Architecture is the oldest interaction design discipline. Unfortunately, it does not yet have a lot of experience with technology, media and their specific requirements. I strongly believe that digital interaction will increasingly be either constrained to very small devices or become part of environments. I am very interested in using space and movement in space, *i.e.* traditional behaviour understood by architects, as ways of interaction. I think the most successful applications in the stores, the magic mirror and the Privalite wall in Prada's Beverly Hills Epicenter Store, are based on interactions that only involve body movements and result in a playful, spontaneous interaction. Whenever customers need to interact with a screen, or even worse with a menu, their interest is lost rapidly.'

The Prada stores, for many, symbolize the marriage between retail and technology. What has been your participation in it and what were the key concepts that you developed? Also, what was the relationship with IDEO?

'Our interaction and collaboration with Prada was very stimulating because of Miuccia Prada's strong desire to develop the brand's store concept and revolutionize the current perception of retailing. I was heading the research and concept team at OMA at the time. After the stores had been conceptualized, our focus turned to the technology and communications aspect of the project. We invited Reed Kram, who I knew from our studies in Boston, to join us. Together with the creative and technical input from the Prada Group, we defined most of the elements of the store scenario.

We found RFID technology very exciting, as it seemed to promise that physical objects and digital information could seamlessly interact. In our scenarios, information would not be carried around. It would, rather, follow customers and staff to wherever they needed it – displays then became part of the environment rather than part of a device. We conceptualized hanging displays, like garments on hangers that would slide in between clothes hanging on a hangbar. They were still connected to the store system and therefore part of an overall scenario. We were interested in going beyond the simple corporate video playing on a screen. Our displays can be activated by a staff device to show movies, fashion shows or information about a specific product. Later on, Clemens Weisshaar gave these displays a beautiful form. Information was to be managed by the staff through a personal device. Only in specific cases would the customer interact directly with it. The dressing rooms, for example, would provide information and have some sort of digital mirror.

IDEO helped in creating the magic mirror with the idea of elastic time even though the first full-scale demo software was written by Reed Kram. They developed the staff device that, in the New York concept, was the mediator between all the different elements of the scenario. And they were instrumental in implementing the RFID technology as that was, at the time, fairly experimental. When we worked on the second store, technology was already so much further advanced that we could work with much more reliable RFID technology. In addition, the application could be reduced to one flexible and versatile piece of .net software, while the New York store was still based on a server system that mediated between different applications. Thanks to the expertise and valuable contribution of Prada Group IT, we no longer needed the support of IDEO.'

A textbook example of how big a media buzz could be generated from the marriage between high-profile architect and fashion brand, the collaboration between Miuccia Prada and Rem Koolhaas' Office for Metropolitan Architecture (OMA) set international press tongues wagging way before any visualization was even rendered 3D. In spring 1999 Prada asked OMA to develop a unified concept for major outlets in New York, Los Angeles, San Francisco and Tokyo. Prada wanted to create a new retail experience for its customers, something that would reflect the company's credo in shopping 'as a singular experience in which culture and consumerism flow together'. Prada also commissioned Swiss architects Herzog & de Meuron and the Japanese Kazuyo Sejima + Ryue Nishizawa to build stores around the globe.

Following the high-profile opening of the New York Prada Epicenter by OMA in 2002 and the Tokyo Aoyama Epicenter by Herzog & de Meuron in 2003, the Los Angeles store by OMA opened in July 2004. All the stores are defined by the integration of retail and performance space, with an innovative employment of technology. Set in Beverly Hills' Rodeo Drive, the favourite hangout for shopping celebrities, the LA store is a total of 2,230 square metres (24,000 square feet) with 1,370 square metres (14,750 square feet) of retail space on three floors. Inside, are housed the ready-to-wear mens and womens collections, the sports line, handbags, shoes, accessories and beauty.

The absence of a façade and of a logo is arguably the LA store's most defining characteristic. The entire 15-metre (50-foot) width opens up onto the street without a traditional, glass-enclosed storefront, which invites the public to enter the building and creates a continuum between the outside and inside. At night, an aluminum wall is raised to hermetically seal the interior. Inside, the store's architecture remains 'uncovered'. Thanks to the meticulous engineering of Arup, the space is

2

1

1 The Prada façade on Rodeo Drive opens up to the street and merges public with commercial space. Invisible security antennas guarantee the safety of the goods inside.

2 Inside the store, a large wooden stair forms a hill-like structure that supports an aluminium box that floats above the entrance. The stair is framed with laminated glass that fades from translucent to transparent.

an interesting mix of column-free space and certain areas where the structure is exposed. Built using a steel brace frame that features special steel trusses, the building has sheer concrete and the floors are steel, framed with composite metal deck and concrete. One of the most notable structural aspects was the design for the roof, which has a steel frame that supports an all-glass, pitched roof. This also doubles as the seismic-resisting diaphragm.

An oval section arch, faced with polished stainless steel, is hollowed out from the double-sided wood staircase at the centre and contains a replica of the first Prada store opened in Milan in 1913, a poignant reference to the company's growth and development. Surfaces are tactile and ingenious – the staircase is framed with laminated glass that fades from translucent to transparent, shoppers sit on gel-like cushions and the aluminium box that floats above the entrance is lined with a spongy, porous material specifically developed for Prada.

Like the New York Epicenter, interactive technology is key to the shopping experience. Each dressing room is a simple 0.74-square-metre (eight-square-foot) booth with Privalite glass walls that switch from transparent to translucent when a room is occupied. Once inside,

the customer can switch the doors back to transparent at the touch of a button, thus exposing themselves to the onlookers waiting outside the room. Different lighting conditions allow customers to view their selections in a warm evening glow or cool blue daylight. IDEO led the design and development of the interactive dressing rooms, working in close collaboration with OMA and AMO, the research branch of OMA.

The elevator features a series of small, LCD screens, integrated into the cabin that scan virtual imagery while the elevator travels through the shaft. Ubiquitous displays, plasma screens built into the furniture or hung between the merchandise, show news feeds and stock market data. The technology here is designed to work in an non-obtrusive and functional way, as well as helping Prada portray itself as a brand with a deep engagement in current cultural context.

4

5

3 Half matter, half air, the spongy material, specifically developed for Prada, provides a porous, artificial background for the merchandise.

4 The wooden staircase is a novel and open-plan means of display. Here, dismembered legs perch on the display boxes modelling a selection of shoes.

5 The roof structure, spanning the entire floor space, admits daylight to the 'scenario-space', where merchandise is arranged within an open, flexible floor plan.

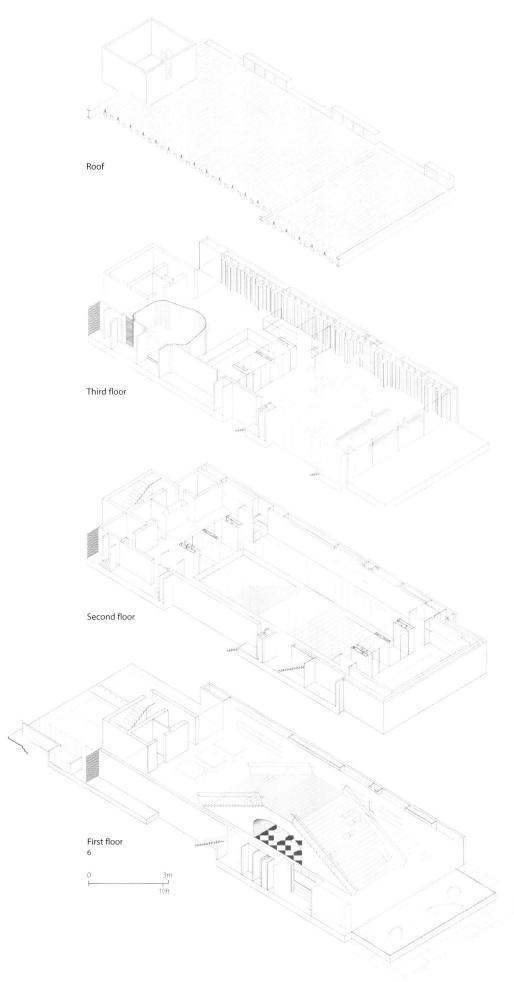

Roof

Third floor

Second floor

First floor
6

0   3m
      10ft

7

6 An axonometric diagram of the building, showing the placement of the alcove beneath the stair-hill.

7 In the mirrored alcove beneath the stair-hill, the black and white marble floor and the vitrines make reference to the first Prada store that was founded in Milan in 1913.

8 Section through the alcove, with stairs above.

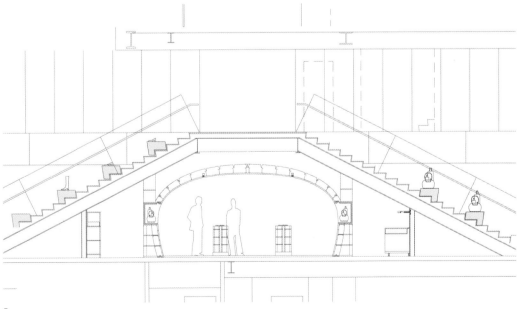

7

1

Multi-awarded retail concept oki-ni brought new meaning to the introduction of technology into retail. With no display rails, no till or obvious signage, oki-ni (meaning 'thank you' in Osaka dialect) presents itself as a singular installation concept based on the tactile and social opportunities that shopping can provide. The store was set up by Paddy Meehan, the fashion entrepreneur behind the fashion label Beauty:Beast, where limited-edition clothes are sold alongside niche brands such as Fake London, Evisu and UACT.

6a Architects were briefed to create a simple, stylish environment with organic natural lines that were more 'Badly Drawn Boy' and less 'LTJ Bukem' (low-fi, breezy music as opposed to a harder-edged techno sound). Emphasis was put on evoking a communal, user-friendly space that would have a transient, light and portable feel. Inspiration was drawn from the artist Joseph Beuys, whose love for felt is widely reproduced in the interior scheme, and from the metal sculptures by Richard Serra. The idea was that the space should not feel like a shop, but more like a comfortable social setting in which to appreciate clothes.

oki-ni was designed as a huge tray, made of Russian oak, which sits neatly in the triangular-shaped shop and works both as display and as furniture. Low piles of felt replace the traditional arrangement of shelving, rails and furniture and help to define oki-ni's physical landscape. The sparsely arranged clothes hang on deliberately cheap, bare metal coat hangers. Details are minimized or avoided, the focus is instead on good lighting and a few low displays.

oki-ni proposes itself as just a physical space for the looking, choosing and trying out of clothes. All the other transaction (payment and ordering) can be done online, either on the spot by a shop assistant or from your own computer from a website designed by the 'trendy'

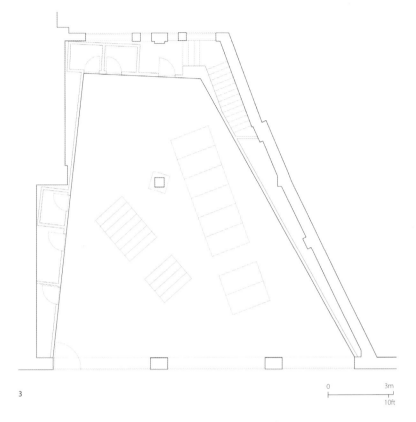

3

0   3m

10ft

2

1 Artist Joseph Beuys and his love of felt were used as inspiration for the sparse interior scheme at oki-ni.

2 oki-ni proposes itself as just the physical space for looking, choosing and trying out clothes. All the economic transactions take place online.

3 The distinctive, triangular floor-plan.

group Fuel. The architects avoided the creation of any point of sale, and proposed the ubiquitous laptop, gently assimilated among the products and visitors, as the sales interface.

The emphasis is not just on online buying, but also on the exclusiveness associated with limited-edition jeans. Against the culture of the quick-fix, power-shopping moment, oki-ni offers individual choice and style, non-conformity and the anticipation that derives from simple waiting (delivery of the final article takes up to three days, no matter what the destination, and can be delivered worldwide). A combination of technology and customization ('rarity is a proof of innocence' reads the epigraph on the oki-ni website) is reinforced by a visual statement similar to the aesthetic of galleries. At oki-ni, the clothes are interspersed with a range of art books and magazines, just like in a museum shop, and display-wise, the hanging items look like they are a part of an art installation or even a project under construction.

6a Architects have an obvious interest in the role of shopping in today's culture. According to them, 'oki-ni is a good example of how the physical environment and a new shopping concept can reinforce each other. oki-ni is a new brand in a world where on-line shopping, traditional shopping, leisure and culture have increasingly overlapped.'

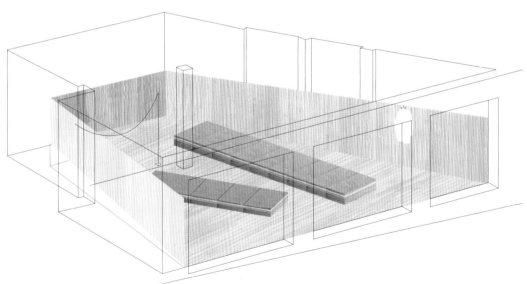

5

4 Designed as a huge oak tray, the layout of oki-ni is both decorative and functional.

5 This computer rendering shows how the oak 'tray' sits in the shop space.

SHOEBALOO

AMSTERDAM/THE NETHERLANDS
MEYER & VAN SCHOOTEN ARCHITECTEN/2003

1

1 The architects chose to design an understated street façade, which employs one-way glass that is only transparent when light is shone behind it.

2 This plan shows the entrance to the right and the egg-shaped display units in the centre.

A designer-footwear chain, specializing in labels such as Prada, Gucci and Fendi, Shoebaloo prizes itself for its constantly cutting-edge interiors. The original retail concept for the site, located in P.C. Hooftstraat, was created 12 years ago by Czech designer Borek Sipek. Looking for something new, the client commissioned Amsterdam-based Meyer & Van Schooten Architecten to recreate the interior.

Contrary to the many boutiques now present on chic P.C. Hooftstraat, Shoebaloo has no clear display window in a deliberate, reverse attempt to intrigue and attract passers-by. Behind the dark mirror-glass of the display windows only glimpses of a few pairs of shoes, illuminated by spotlights, are visible. The reflective front door mirrors the street and the passers-by, with the intention of stopping them on their steps and luring them inside. The dark façade contrasts with the wildly illuminated inside.

As the mirror doors slide open, the shop interior reveals itself as a futuristic, styled environment, set within a nineteenth-century building. Inside, vacuum-moulded, translucent polyacrylic is used for the ceiling and for wall-mounted shelving that contains niches for the display of

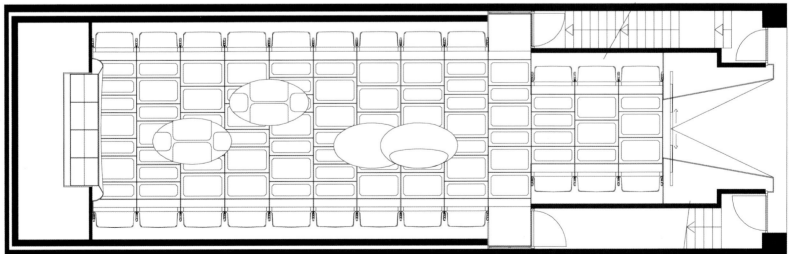

shoes. The floor is glass, underneath which sits more polyacrylic panels. Because of the lighting and the reflections of the mirrors at the front of the shop, the depth of the actual space is difficult to grasp.

The egg-shaped display units for accessories are complemented by egg-shaped furniture (two benches and a counter) painted in glossy white paint. Situated behind the shells of all the plastic panels are 540 fluorescent light tubes that create an artificial atmosphere. The colour pattern of the lighting scheme can be changed by the retailer via a computer system. Slow-changing patterns or static configurations can bathe areas of the shop in pink, blue, red or green.

Tones can also be varied at the same time with, for example, a blue light glowing at the front of the store and a red one at the back. The colour change can take about five minutes or even less. Following the success of this Amsterdam shop, the architects are about to design another Shoebaloo, this time in Rotterdam.

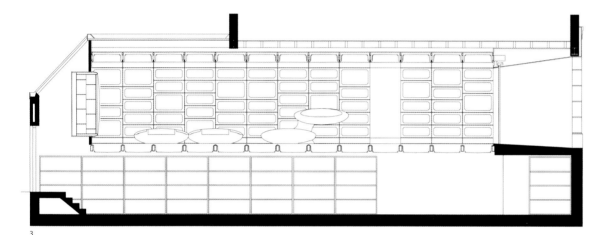
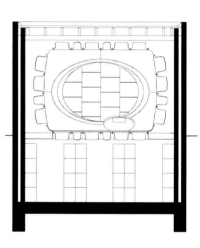

3

4

5

6

7

3 From left: long and short section plans of the shop.

4 The computer-controlled lighting can be set to a series of slowly changing patterns or configured to remain static.

5 The futuristic looking pieces of furniture are seats, a cash desk and display cases for accessories.

6 The floor is made of glass, underneath which sit more acrylic panels.

7 Inside the shop, vacuum-moulded translucent, polyacrylic is used for the ceiling and wall-mounted shelving, with niches for the display of shoes.

Ron Arad's product-design background and penchant for audacious technological innovations that act both as solutions as well as cheerful provocations is well-represented in Y's. In 2002, London-based Ron Arad Associates (RAA) was approached by fashion designer Yohji Yamamoto to design the new Tokyo's flagship store for the company's 'Y's' label. When presenting the preliminary sketches and ideas, RAA was given carte blanche to design the store, while keeping within the constraints of the budget and the physical characteristics of the site. The building of the Y's store coincided with the label's total brand revamp, one that included the way in which the clothes were sold in retail environments.

The store occupies a 570-square-metre (6,135-square-foot) area, divided by three large structural columns. RAA masked the columns in a way that would create an illusion of lightness and movement within the space. Strong reference was drawn from the mechanical automobile parking turntables that are common in Tokyo. The three existing columns,

1

plus a 'fake' one, were transformed into sculptures resembling the turntables, and embedded into the floor. Each of these rotating, industrial-looking sculptures is made of 34 tubular, aluminium loops, stacked to occupy the entire distance between the floor and the ceiling around steel column casings – they act almost as structural supports. In fact, the store ceiling and floor appear to be almost held apart by these four, ever-changing elements.

Each of these loops can be rotated 360 degrees, accommodating an infinite number of spatial arrangements. The gentle pirouettes of the sculptures create a flexible environment, one in which the store reconfigures itself several times during a visit. As the customers peruse within this fluid structure, they hardly notice the slow movement of the sculptures, but when the shop closes, the speed of the rotation accelerates, via a lever, with the turntables spinning like the inside of a washing machine. The loops are used as shop-fitting elements. Within the stacks of lozenge-shaped rings, each element can rotate individually to create a rail for Y's clothes. They can also be transformed into wide shelves using special customized 'plug-in' units, and acquire a decorative function as objects are hung on them.

Additional product display units are made from a series of angular glass-fibre, reinforced plastic shelves that can dock into each other to form free-standing shelf stacks. The till is formed by a series of displaced, identical, angular plates that mimic both the shelves and the rotating loops. The changing rooms are located behind gill-like curved walls, and coloured LED lights tell customers whether the room is occupied or not. Outside, the façade is made of a series of curved glass panels forming a refractory glass surface that, when looked through, distorts and stretches the contents of the store. The revolving store entrance door is decorated with the freehand letters 'Y' and 'S'; they had first appeared in Arad's preliminary sketches and ended up becoming the store's logo. When the door is spun open, they shimmer and change colour.

1 The street-facing façade is composed of an array of curved glass panels forming a refractory glass structure that distorts and stretches the contents of the store from the outside.

2 The revolving store entrance is adorned with four layers of coloured glass pieces, forming a freehand Y's logo that, when the door is spun, shimmers and changes colour.

3

4

3 The large structural columns have been masked with tubular aluminium loops to become both decorative and functional elements of the store.

4 These sculptural elements are made of 34 aluminium, tubular loops, stacked to occupy the entire distance between the floor and the ceiling.

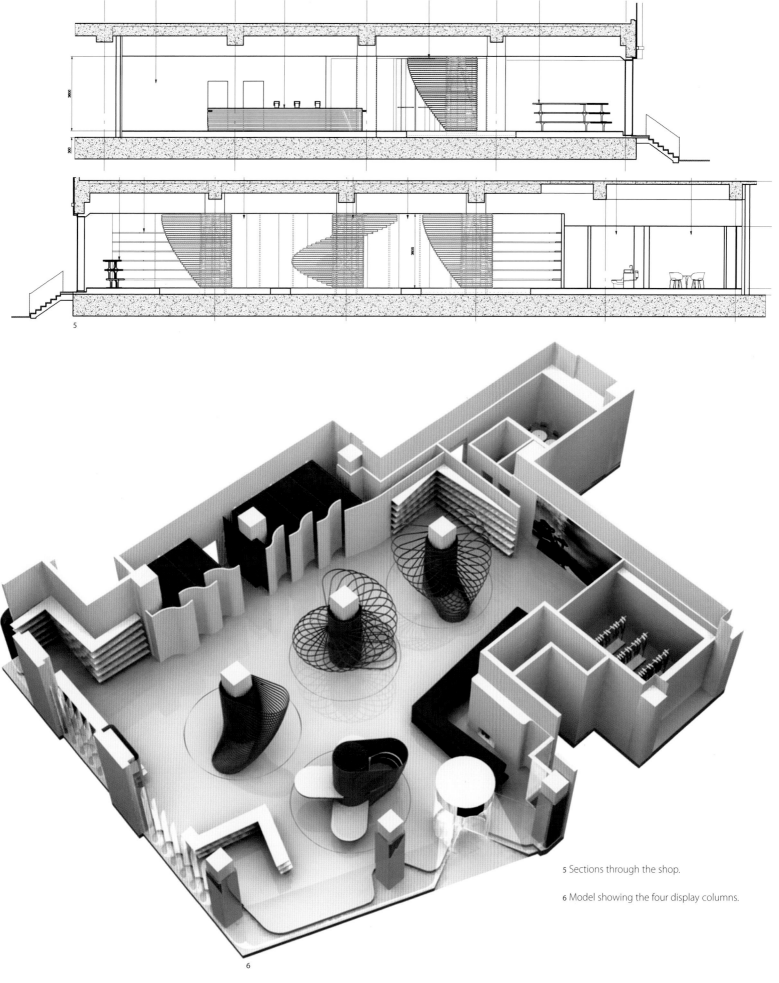

5 Sections through the shop.

6 Model showing the four display columns.

The Tokyo HQ for the Italian shoe and bag brand Tod's is situated on the tree-lined Omotesando Avenue. Architect Toyo Ito drew on the surrounding trees for inspiration when he was designing the distinctive concrete façade, seen here from inside the store.

FASHIONABLE STOPOVERS

INTRODUCTION

The love affair between fashion designers and high-profile architects is a commercial fairy tale made in creative heaven. Fashion stores need cultural kudos in a bid to justify their existence, and architects are only too happy to indulge in the ephemeral world of fashion. Retail projects allow for an open brief and superior budgets and they are often perceived as great ways to experiment, the results of which generate worldwide curiosity and concentrated media attention. From John Pawson's minimalist retail temple for Calvin Klein, designed in New York in 1996, to Armani's commissions of Claudio Silvestrin and Massimiliano and Doriana Fuksas, there are very few names that have not been involved in this particular pastime. Even the younger generation of achingly hip fashion designers like Stella McCartney and Alexander McQueen are keen to sign up their own personal architect who can embody their stylish, image-conscious brands.

Designer Rei Kawakubo, who founded Comme des Garçons in 1973, was one the first to initiate the cross-pollination between the two camps. In 1998 she commissioned Future Systems to design her store in New York. Since then, Future Systems has worked with several fashion retailers, such as the Italian retailer Marni, the British fashion chain New Look and the British department store Selfridges. Amanda Levete, of Future Systems, talks about the practice's projects and how shops have become 'fashionable stopovers'.

How did the relationship with Rei Kawakubo work?

'She is an amazing character, both an artist and the head of a fashion empire. However well she is doing, every ten years she reinvents herself. We did three shops for Comme des Garçons. The New York store (1998) was a rare piece of industrial heritage located in the West Chelsea area, then associated more with art galleries than shops. Rather than refurbish the whole structure, we decided to keep the 1950s' feel of it and designed a transition from the outside to the inside, which was an aluminium tunnel that swept you in. With the Tokyo one (1998), which was a smaller space set within a 1970s' office building, we reduced the size of the entrance and replaced it with inclined curved patterned glass, so as to give it a tunnel effect. The façade was a series of large panels of glass covered with spotted film. In 1999, for the Parfum Shop in Place des Vosges in Paris, we had to work within the restrictions of a nineteenth-century listed apartment building. The question here was how do you transform the perception of a building? We decided to do it through large, flat sheets of coloured glass attached with bolts: both a soft and powerful graphic device. The colour decreases in intensity as it rises up the façade, allowing the original stone front to show through.'

You were at that time approached by Marni, an Italian fashion label only known by the style conscious few.

'For Marni, we created the first flagship store in London and then in Milan, Paris and New York. We needed to reflect the romantic nature of the brand, hence the space could not be another minimalist shop. With London, we came up with this idea of the shop as a landscape. We wanted to get away from the traditional concept of having clothes on rails, so we designed a system in which the clothes were suspended from the ceiling. By creating abstract forms, the clothes worked as artwork, invisibly framed by a romantic landscape.'

Then Vittorio Radice, then chief executive of Selfridges, asked you to build a new department store in Birmingham.

'We had always dreamt of doing something big. Radice had seen the NatWest Media Centre at Lord's Cricket Ground in London. Completed in 1999, the small, streamlined aluminium pod had won architecture's RIBA Stirling Prize. He told us he wanted us to do something for the city of Birmingham. The site was an example of terrible postwar planning and needed some real regeneration. In order for Selfridges to work in Birmingham, it had to do something in a scale that would change the perception of the city. The issue was how to clad a largely opaque building in an affordable way that could turn a doubly curved corner. We looked at fashion influences like Paco Rabanne, we looked at animals and fish scales, and we even looked at baroque churches and how, historically, they have managed to break down mass via plastered forms. Finally we came up with the notion of polished, anodized, aluminium discs. They are a successful device because they really catch the light.'

Your mark was largely on the exterior with the curvaceous shape and the 15,000 anodized aluminum disks, but there is also a striking interior and other designers have been involved in different floors and their concessions.

'Once you have set up such an expectation from the outside, you have to match it on the inside. Each designer was allocated a floor; we chose the food hall downstairs. We strived to do enough for the interior that would hold it all together. For the atrium, we wanted to get away from the department store cliché of the escalator and glass façade. We clad the escalators in matt white plaster to make them more muscular and sensuous. It was important to emphasize the theatricality and the drama of the atrium. We also thought that the rooflight was very important. Often in department stores you have a roof that is illuminated with artificial light; for us it was important to give a sense of the outside, the weather and the clouds. Another important element was the store's relationship with the sixteenth-century church, Saint Martin's, next door. The store is conceived as a backdrop to the church and the juxtaposition works very well. You understand better the scale of the store by seeing it next to another building.'

And of course there is the now the common association of shops being the new churches.

'The church used to be the meeting place, and now the department store is the great meeting place. But the relationship between the two spaces in Birmingham is real, the local priest even organizes a shoppers' service on Sunday.'

Much has been said about shops being a fashionable stopover – not just because of the merchandise, but also because they are spaces that people want to visit with an architectural value and fascination of their own. Some critics have even compared the way museums like the Guggenheim use architecture to attract visitors to commercial brands such as Coca-Cola.

'I'm very wary of these comparisons. Buildings take about four years to complete while a shop is complete within months. They are much more experimental, temporary, and you are constantly going out of fashion. Also, the Bilbao Guggenheim had millions spent on it. Selfridges was built with a developer's budget for the same cost per square metre as the Debenhams store next door, which does not have cultural ambitions. Yet it has become an iconic building, so much so that even Selfridges' store card has the Birmingham building on it as a logo. Selfridges was about selling, but figures says that over 100 million people a year pass by the London store, which is way more than Tate Modern art gallery. It really makes you ask: What is the nature of a public building? Is it visual? Is it creative? Is it an experience?'

ALEXANDER MCQUEEN

NEW YORK/USA

WILLIAM RUSSELL/2002

1

1 A series of columns, rooted in the terrazzo flooring, define the space of the store while display shelves are carved out of the curvaceous walls.

2 Alexander McQueen's store in the meat-packing district in New York has a simple, clean façade.

3 Long sections through the sides and centre of the shop.

Enfant prodige Alexander McQueen joined forces with architect and friend William Russell, now a partner at Pentagram in London, for his New York flagship store on West 14th Street, which is set to become the blueprint for future stores in London and Milan. Like Stella McCartney and Universal Design Studio (pages 82–85), and Chloé and Sophie Hicks, the personal, ongoing collaboration between a designer and a hip young architect becomes more than just a commission; it is proof that they are ahead of the pack.

A constant personal collaboration is also seen as the most creative way in which the ephemeral nature of fashion can feed off the more cerebral kudos of architecture. Like fellow designer McCartney, McQueen also chose New York's meat-packing district to feature his women's ready-to-wear, accessories and shoes, in an attempt to divert the shopper's attention from more conventional sites like Madison Avenue.

Together with Russell, McQueen articulated his vision with what he likens to the levitating spaceship from the film *Close Encounters of the Third Kind*. The store's interior is a glowing, otherworldly white and pale gray cocoon of softly rounded curves and coves; there are very few angles of any kind. The New York store's focus of attention is the ceiling, from which huge columns and other sculptural forms descend and root themselves to the terrazzo floor. The 38,750-square-metre (3,600-square-foot) space unveils itself as a crisp, glacier-like environment. A 30-centimetre- (one-foot-) wide stripe of light, embedded in the walls, gives either an all-white reflection or a greenish-blue hue. The space feels as if it has been hollowed out of a solid block rather than constructed piece by piece. The walls curve seamlessly into the ceiling, which in turn forms floating display cabinets that look as if they have also been carved from the same homogenous block.

At the centre of the store is 'The Mother Ship' structure, a ghostly ovoid island of sculpted plaster rising from the pearlized terrazzo floor. The structure holds three fitting rooms in elegant walnut veneer as well as a Victorian cut-glass box where couture items are exhibited. Made of hemispheric shelves, the box recalls a windowed mosque, adding a touch of exoticism to the cool and collected interior. Various hanging McQueen creations and sculptural mannequins contribute to the dreamy atmosphere of the space. From the outside, the lit façade stands discreetly signposted.

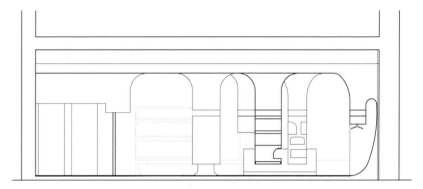

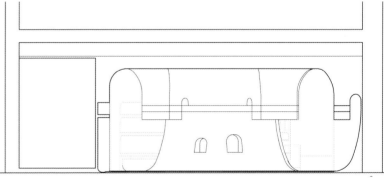

2

3

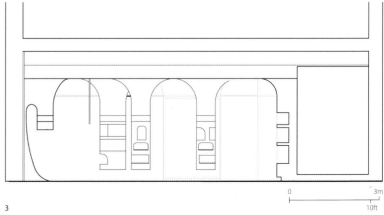

0 3m
10ft

4

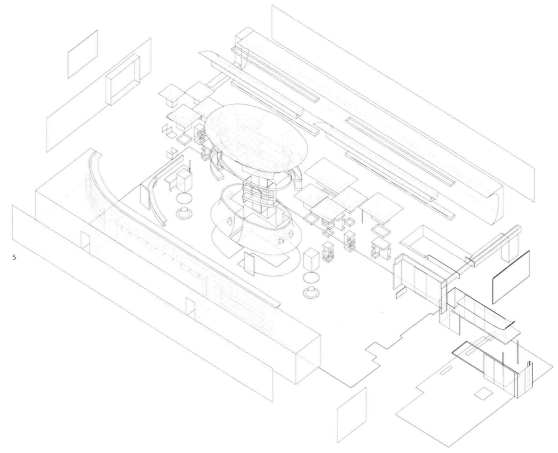

5

6

4 A large ovoid structure, dubbed the 'Mother Ship', functions as the main decorative element in the shop.

5 An exploded axonometric diagram shows the structure of the central ovoid 'Mother Ship'.

6 Wide strips of lighting, embedded in the walls, give the display units and the clothes either a white reflection or a greenish-blue hue.

Taking its cue from the Armani, Milan megastore, an 8,000-square-metre (86,110-square-foot) retail centre, that opened in 2000 and sells all the Armani clothes and accessories lines under one roof) the fashion label repeated the formula in 2002 by opening a 2,000-square-metre (21,530-square-foot) Armani in Hong Kong. Retail-wise, Hong Kong is the perfect springboard from which to conquer China and it appeals to the conspicuous consumption habits of Hong Kong dwellers.

In contrast with the pared-down architectural style of the Italian Claudio Silvestrin, who designed the main body of the five-storey building, Chater House, the Giorgio Armani boutique on the ground floor and the accessories area on the first floor, Rome-based Massimiliano and Doriana Fuksas were commissioned to design a fresher, funkier look for the Emporio Armani store.

According to Massimiliano and Doriana Fuksas, the Emporio Armani project in Hong Kong was born with the insight that 'global culture is an experimental territory of many identities. It is the encounter of diverse modes of sensing the world…' The whole project developed around the idea of fluidity, inspired by the casual movements of visitors and customers. The space was thus conceived as a stage, where the visitor is both the actor and the protagonist of a very special experience.

The result is a store in which the space is filled with lightness, owing mainly to the floor of blue-coloured epoxy resin that shimmers like water and is reflected by the glass-reinforced gypsum ceiling. The bespoke

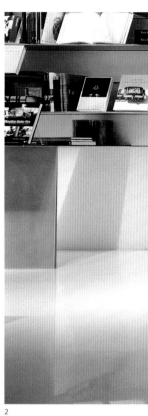

2

1

1 The blue-tinged, epoxy resin floor, reflected by the glass-reinforced gypsum ceiling, gives the store a sense of lightness and fluidity.

2 All the satin stainless-steel display tables and units are designed by Massimiliano and Doriana Fuksas and manufactured by Zeus.

furniture, made of sheets of stainless steel and clad in soft, translucent Plexiglas, reinforces the sense of weightlessness. The merchandise is displayed in sleek, suspended glass boxes or on pared-down clothes rails.

The main feature of the space is the undulating, red fibreglass ribbon that runs through the store, creating a route among the shop, the café, the bookshop, the florist and the cosmetic department. In the restaurant, the ribbon transforms itself into a bar table, rising and dropping to create a dining space, it then transforms into a DJ booth, then into a bar space and finally spirals into a tunnel to form the main entrance to the store. In the bar area, the ribbon is matched by a luminescent curving strip on the ceiling that almost creates the effect of a motorcar ramp. Inspired by the spiralling coloured ribbons used by Chinese gymnasts, the red colour is also a precise cultural reference to China, where it means happiness. Outside, the façade is also decorated by an illuminated red dragon-like motif, which changes intensity to reflect the pulsing life of Hong Kong. These details are a radical departure from the neutral-toned world of Giorgio Armani, but one that works wonders in creating a spectacular retail environment.

3

4

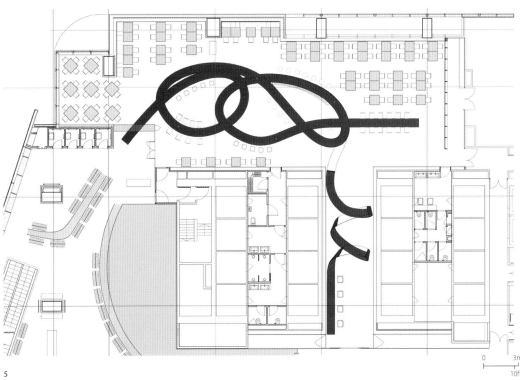

5

3 The red fibreglass ribbon twirls around the store to define the space and accentuate different areas.

4 The red ribbon is inspired by the spiralling, coloured ribbons of Chinese gymnasts and is also a direct reference to China, where red means happiness.

5 Plan: shoppers follow the red fibreglass ribbon through the entrance corridor (bottom right) into the main store.

This is a typical representation of the 'boutique palazzo' style that is increasingly becoming a feature for high-end fashion-brand architecture. This flagship store for Christian Dior, created by Japanese architectural practice SANAA, is situated on Omotesando Street in Tokyo, an area largely devoted to luxury shopping. It is no coincidence that on the same street Tod's building (pages 86–91), designed by architect Toyo Ito, has also recently opened. Unlike other commissions, the boutique palazzo approach focuses on the façade of the building, leaving the design and shop fitting of the interiors to in-house teams.

SANAA, the practice of Kazuyo Sejima and Ryue Nishizawa is, at the moment, arguably one of the most fashionable in Japan, having also just completed the 21st Century Museum of Contemporary Art, Kanazawa, and being currently involved in building the Valencia Institute of Modern Art. Their brief was to create a shop from basement through to third floor with a multipurpose room on the fourth floor. SANAA decided to focus on the façade, one that would show the interior and, at the same time, offer a cohesive image for the building. The entire façade is covered with flat glass, making the whole building transparent. The transparency is controlled by an interior layer of gently curved acrylic, reminiscent of the flowing folds in Dior's couture dresses. The transparency of the building means that the customers and the clothes are almost placed upon a stage. On the fourth floor the beauty parlour appears as an art installation, with a luminescent forest of upside-down lanterns hanging from the ceiling. The large logo of Dior on the façade further reinforces the idea of the building as the brand messenger.

1

1 The transparency of the façade is Dior, Tokyo's most defining feature. It is made possible by an interior layer of gently curved acrylic, positioned behind the glass, and is reminiscent of the flowing folds in Dior's dresses.

2

3

2 Set in busy Omotesando Street, the structure takes advantage of Tokyo's height regulations for buildings.

3 At night, the glowing skin of the façade turns the building into an ideal brand messenger.

4

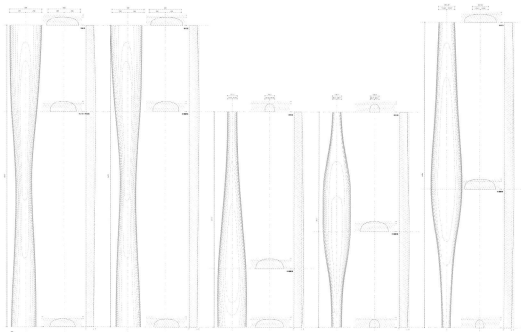
5

4 The architectural practice SANAA was commissioned to focus on the façade of the building, leaving the interiors and shop fitting to Dior's in-house teams.

6

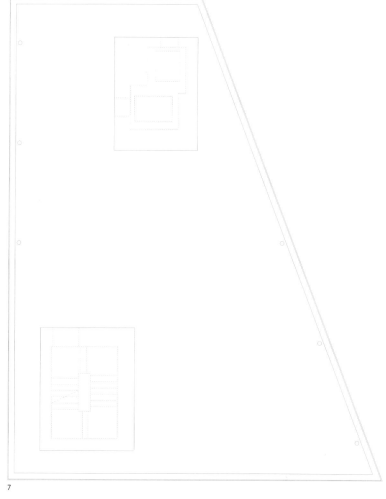

7

The site was constrained by being located within a restricted building area, which had very tall maximum height regulations. The regulated maximum building height is at a ratio of five to one with the maximum floor area. SANAA chose to emphasize both characteristics by creating many floors with different heights and uses – some for shopping, others for events. High ceilings have the effect of making the rooms seem more spacious. In a city like Tokyo where space is so restricted and public areas are not constituted, like in European cities, by a piazza, retail flagships have to work extra hard to make themselves noticed, often on busy, narrow streets. The skin of the building and the outside exterior become defining elements of the growing metropolis.

The imposing silhouette of the simple glass sheath with white horizontals is given even more emphasis by the proximity of a traditional Japanese building next door. At night, the Dior Building is lit and becomes an ethereal, white, glowing city landmark.

5 A drawing of the undulating acrylic interior façade.

6 The high ceilings in the store have the effect of making the room appear more spacious.

7 The building's unusual footprint was dictated by the site and by strict height regulations.

Founded by Eduardo Fendi, the Fendi sisters have been crafting fashion, accessories and furs since 1925, but it was third-generation family member Silvia Venturini, Fendi's creative director, who put the brand on the global map by creating a status symbol for the fashion world, such as the 'Baguette Bag'. Venturini has also been the mind behind the company's new worldwide retail strategy, executed by Rome-based architects Lazzarini Pickering in cities such as Rome, Paris, London and New York.

Located near the elegant shopping heaven of Avenue Montaigne, the Paris store strives hard to stand out amid its luxurious neighbours. While aiming to be immediately recognizable, it was designed to create a unique spatial and shopping experience as well as a space that is reflective of local architectural traditions and materials.

1

2

The entire boutique revolves around the spatial device of a staircase, which is a vortex of sculptural display elements that encourages the shopper to use all of the floors. Three floors are connected by the open staircase in a geometric game of square shapes that spiral towards the top. The shelves, tables and horizontal and vertical hanging fascias are of an architectural scale and proportionate to the space. The shelves are up to 10 meters (33 feet) long; the tables are 7 metres (23 feet) and the hanging fascias up to 20 meters (66 feet) long. Luxurious bags are displayed as if they are in a void, their preciousness heightened by a system of indirect lighting. Clothes are hung or laid out in an informal way – the carefully conceived 'disorder' of the display encourages clients to touch the precious materials and try on the various pieces.

The use of traditional and humble, low-tech materials has provided the opportunity to try out new finishes. Rough, rendered surfaces are finished with a ferromicaceous paint that is normally employed to protect metal surfaces. The crude iron is first treated with a nitrate solvent, to make it virtually stainless, and then it is wax-finished. This in some way reflects Fendi's unconventional attitude towards furs and leathers, both in the treatment and manufacture as well as the combination with other materials.

Following the current retail trend that sees a departure from chilly minimalism as a style that does not encourage shopping or experience, the architects have created an interior palette that is warm with natural grey timber tones, shades of grey, brown and black. The Fendi image is projected as dark, architectural and luxurious.

1 The dark-toned décor offsets the bright garments and accessories on display.

2 The raw steel shelves and wenge tables were designed by the architects.

3

3 Accessories are displayed in a sculptural way, in keeping
with the shop's 3D configuration of shelves, hanging
systems and tables.

4

5

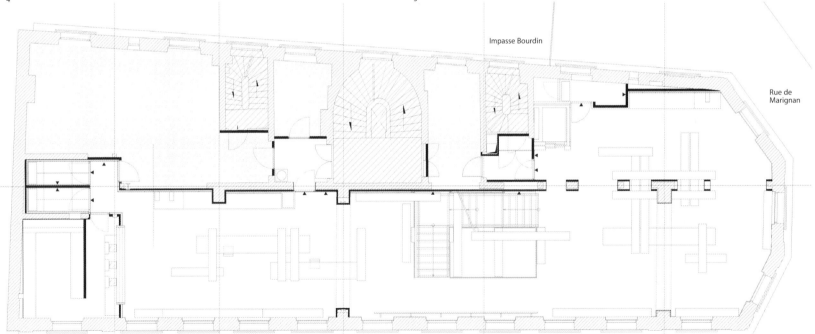

6

4 The entire store's space revolves around the staircase, which acts as a vortex of sculptural display elements.

5 For the Paris store, the crude iron was treated with a nitrate solvent and then wax-finished.

6 Second-floor plan.

Impasse Bourdin

Rue de Marignan

Gallery, a luxury shoe and accessories boutique on Andorra's main shopping boulevard, is aimed at an exclusive clientele who are keen to keep the environment relaxed. Pons recalls, 'We wanted to avoid the hands-off atmosphere that customers experience in certain Gucci shops, for example. Some shops try so hard to be exquisite that they become tense spaces with no sense of human warmth.'

In order to achieve this warmth, Pons has used pale wood for the main staircase and for the wall panels, cabinets and fittings, with pale-green upholstery on seats and benches. The designer's biggest challenge was to make the three-storey space with low ceilings seem light and open. To remedy any sense of claustrophobia, large openings were punched in the ceilings and floors. A wide staircase with a nautical-style white, tubular handrail connects all three levels. Highly varnished surfaces

1

1 Pale wood for the wall panels, cabinets and fittings conveys a sense of warmth and lightness to the space.

2 Specially designed sales assistant stations are set flush into mirror-panelled walls so that they do not intrude onto the shop floor.

3 Mirrors, lighting and openings in the low ceiling increase the perception of space.

2

bounce the light around, while mirrored panels increase the sense of space. The effect is at once low-key and luxurious.

To increase the sense of space in the store, storage and display areas are recessed into the wall spaces. Specially designed assistants' stations, boxes in sleek, shiny black lacquer, are set into mirrored wall panels for minimal intrusion into the calm shopping environment.

4 Green upholstery and pale wood create a low-key, but luxurious, environment.

3

4

According to Selfridges marketing director, James Bidwell, the store in Birmingham was conceived as a place for cutting-edge individuals to gather and socialize, as well as to shop. The $66.4 million department store was built as the centrepiece of a $750 million redevelopment of the Bull Ring – an area that comprises 16 hectares (40 acres) in the centre of Birmingham. The astounding, armadillo-like building was especially commissioned to rejuvinate people's opinion of the city.

The brainchild of Vittorio Radice, then MD of Selfridges, who notoriously defined the department store as a 'house of brands' and the shopping experience as 'theatre', the Birmingham site was conceived by London-based architects Future Systems. Radice's brief was to create a building that would change the perception of the city.

The actual store is 23,230 square metres (250,000 square feet). The building is curvilinear with no windows, but with a stunning, royal blue outer shell. The exterior surface is covered with 15,000 anodized aluminium discs that create an almost snake-like appearance. This cladding solved the issue of how to turn a doubly curved corner while also being economically sustainable. The discs create a fine, lustrous grain, like the sequins on a Paco Rabanne dress. Above, a sky bridge takes

2

1

1 The striking silhouette of the Birmingham Selfridges stands out against the city's skyline and provides an excellent contrast to St. Martin's Church next door.

2 The store consists of various floors offering fashion, food, homeware, technology and beauty products.

3 Fifteen thousand anodized aluminium discs applied to the stone façade create and armadillo-like appearance.

3

4

5

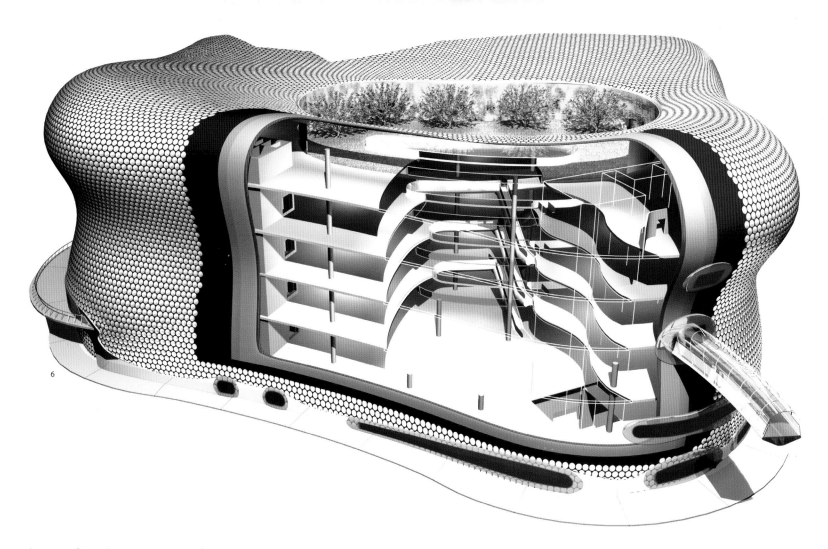

shoppers from the store into an adjacent multi-storey car park. Future Systems chose to illustrate its curvaceous and organic style by making the bridge curved rather than straight; support for it comes from cables attached to a single point on the store's exterior.

Inside, according to Future Systems' partner Amanda Levete, 'circulation was the key' as well as the need to maximize accessibility on every level so that no floor would dominate another. The most spectacular element of the asymmetric interior is the atrium, with its high-gloss white balconies and dizzying array of escalators, recalling a vast skeletal structure. The escalators are clad in robust white plaster, making them sculptural rather than just functional. A glass rooftop allows natural daylight to pour down into the great, canted atrium and gives a clear view of the sky, giving a real sense of the weather conditions outside.

The store has seven floors, four of which are devoted to retail. A different designer was involved in each floor: Milan-based Aldo Cibic and Partners for the fourth and top retail floor; Staunton Williams for the third level; the second was by London-based Eldridge Smerin and the lower

level, comprising the food hall, was by Future Systems themselves. Here one can find over ten 'eatover' counters, serving Indian, Japanese and Italian cuisine, among others, and a wine department.

The technology department on the second floor features green rubber floors and walls that are made of expanded foam. Also on the second floor, several brands live in differently designed concessions. The overall look and feel is provided by exposed metalwork, a seamless poured-resin floor and silver photographers' reflectors overhead. The third floor features the menswear department and includes a dark-gray resin floor and an exposed ceiling with overhead cable trays. The top floor, set within an ambience of luxury, fitted with carpets, curved walls and a series of split-level zones, houses the Gallery restaurant and a range of international designers names.

4 The focal point of the store is the atrium, with a dizzying array of escalators and high-gloss balconies.

5 The escalators are clad in robust white plaster, turning the functional into the sculptural.

6 A cutaway computer rendering of the building shows how light enters through the roof and floods the central atrium below.

Stella McCartney's propulsion into the 'A-list' world of fashion designers was no doubt helped by the three stores that were designed for her by budding London architectural practice Universal Design Studio, the retail and interiors arm of furniture designers Barber Osgerby. After a stint at Chloé, Stella McCartney went on to create her own fashion brand, a sassy girl-about-town label endorsed by her celebrity friends and characterized by crisp tailoring and a feminine edge.

Her first store was the New York flagship, located in the trendy meat-packing district. The brief to Universal Design Studio was for a relaxed environment with an air of nature, where customers could feel free to explore and discover the ready-to-wear collection. Set in a gritty urban landscape, the environment wanted to evoke an idealized British landscape, a retreat from the humdrum of the city. As with many retailers today, McCartney was also keen to create a distinctive shopping experience that would attract customers: a space that is defined by clean and modern lines while maintaining a 'soft', rather than a tougher technology driven, interior.

Universal Design Studio simplified the brief into four main themes: relaxation, nature, discovery and differentiation. Nature and relaxation were represented by an 'abstract landscape' built in different scales throughout the 372-square-metre (4,000-square-foot) warehouse |space. The window display is set in a pool of water with lily-like display structures – the water reflects the natural light, thus minimizing the reliance on artificial light. Hanging screens, evocative of blades of grass, create partitions and sway in the air as customers come in. The long eastern wall is crafted out of white ceramic 3D hexagonal tiles, designed by Barber Osgerby, cleverly turning the hard material into a delicate pattern. More decoration comes in the guise of the western wall, covered in a peach fabric and prettily outlined by motifs of hummingbirds,

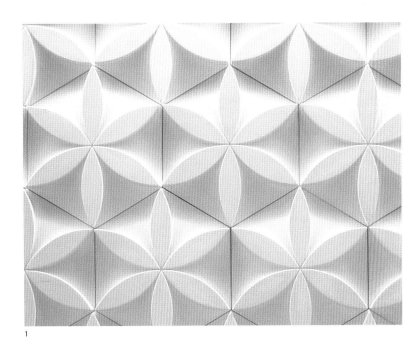

1

2

1 The long eastern wall is crafted out of white ceramic 3D hexagonal tiles.

2 Hanging screens, evocative of blades of grass, introduce the 'nature' theme to the store.

3

4

5

3 The window display is set in a pool of water that reflects the natural light into the shop.

4 Vintage items are cleverly encased in delicate display drawers lined with floral silk inlays.

5 All the furniture in the store is custom-made by Barber Osgerby.

flowers, trees, horseshoes and a female centaur, all designed by McCartney herself.

Other features interpret the differentiation theme. Most of the furniture, display units and hanging rails are flexible and can be rearranged. The rear section is an intimate lounge, featuring bespoke seating by Barber Osgerby that has the period look of mid-century (1950s) pieces. In a bid to remove the financial transaction as much as possible from the shopping experience, the till has been withdrawn from the front of house to a room at the rear where a sales-person conducts all transactions.

Having eliminated the financial aspect, the store's design focuses on emphasizing the social and discovering experience. Customers are encouraged to rummage through several drawers, lined with different floral silk inlays, to discover Stella McCartney's collection of bespoke pieces and vintage finds, such as costume jewellery, accessories and chinaware. Floor-to-ceiling mirrors rotate on their vertical axes, enhancing the spacious atmosphere in a sophisticated game of hide-and-seek.

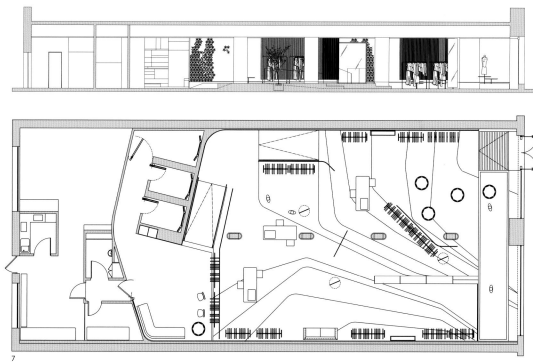

7

6 The themes of 'nature' and 'relaxation' are represented by an abstract landscape built in different scales.

7 From the top: a section and plan showing the varied floor contours in the Stella McCartney store.

TOD'S BUILDING

Italian shoe and bag brand Tod's decided to go for a piece of the Japanese retail cake with its new Tokyo HQ building located on the shopping strip Omotesando Avenue. Here, wedged between the steel spider web of the Prada Epicenter and the crystal waves of Christian Dior (pages 68–71), stands the seven-storey structure. Keen to give Tod's an identity that would make it stand out from the crowd of places devoted to conspicuous consumption, Chairman Diego Della Valle commissioned the Tokyo architect Toyo Ito with the specific brief to employ high quality materials and colours that would reflect Tod's notion of 'naturalness'. The leather-goods brand is well-known for its impeccably handcrafted shoes and bags as well as its great attention to the natural quality of leathers.

The nature metaphor that has been applied to the store was drawn from Omotesando's long row of zelkova trees. According to Toyo Ito, 'The tree is an autonomous, natural object and therefore its shape has an inherent structural rationality. In a sense, producing a reasonable flow of structural loads with a pattern of superimposed tree silhouettes is a result of a perfectly rational thought process'.

The distinctive concrete façade of the building is thus a tree shaped silhouette made of nine overlapping ramifications. Twenty-seven metres (89 feet) high, the enveloping body opens at the side in a corner that leads west. The 2,550 square metres (27,450 square feet) contains retail spaces on the first three levels, offices in part of the third floor and the fourth and fifth levels, a multifunctional space for events on the sixth floor, and a panoramic meeting room on the roof garden.

1

2

1 Toyo Ito drew inspiration for the store's façade from Omotesando Avenue's long row of zelkova trees.

3

2 At night, the lights from within the store illuminate the 'branches', emphasizing the architectural form of the outer skin.

3 The staircase connecting the store's seven floors allows for views of the distinctive structure of the building as well as the outside.

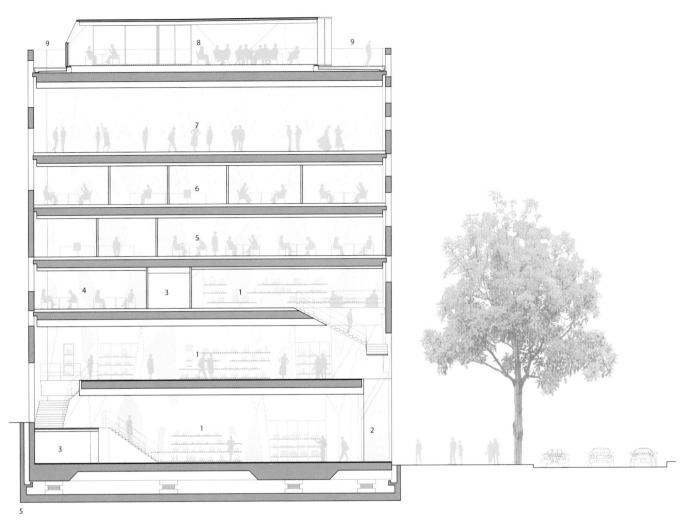

5

Toyo Ito's fondness for the outer skin that wraps a building is once again well-represented. His *pao* (wrap) philosophy underpins much of his work, from the Serpentine Pavilion in Hyde Park, London, that he built in 2002 together with the London-based engineers Arup, to the Sendai Mediatheque in Japan, whose outer surface has been dissolved into thin sheets of glass. With Tod's, the dramatic building's outer skin copies the structure of the tall trees nearby. At night, when the spaces between the 'branches' are lit from within, the architectural and the natural form almost become one.

Inside, the interiors blend Ito's adventurous forms with Tod's classic Italian style. Polished plaster walls and walnut floors provide the setting for the merchandise, while Zaha Hadid's burgundy sofas provide seating; small side tables are where Tod's staff keep their shoehorns. Artificial light is well conceived with warm, golden hues, while the abundance of natural light is due to the total non-obstruction of other buildings on the road. Tod's most celebrated product, the 'Gommino' loafer, is displayed in all its variations, while the third floor is specifically devoted to more precious items such as bags in ostrich and crocodile leather. On the top (seventh) floor, the boardroom features sliding glass doors, padded leather walls and floors clad in marble travertine.

4 The concrete façade reflects architect Toyo Ito's predilection for the outer skin that wraps a building.

5 Cross section through the store: 1. shop, 2. show window, 3. stock room, 4. office, 5. Tod's Japan office, 6. Tod's press office, 7. party space, 8. penthouse, 9. roof garden.

6

6 The interiors blend Toyo Ito's adventurous forms with Tod's classical Italian style.

7 Ground-floor plan: 1. shop, 2. machine room, 3. stock room.

8 Seating by Zaha Hadid and a blend of natural light and warm artificial light create a relaxed setting.

7

1
2
3

8

Luxury fashion came to the Middle East in 2002 the form of Villa Moda, a fashion emporium that holds the world's leading designer brands, including Gucci, Bottega Veneta, Prada and Fendi. It is the brainchild of Sheik Majed al-Sabah, nephew to the emir of Kuwait and an entrepreneur who first started importing American fashion brands in the 1990s. Realizing the huge potential of supplying solvent, fashion-conscious Arab women customers, Sheik Majed first bought an abandoned warehouse in central Kuwait to stock and sell international brands; when the space became too small, he expanded to a larger space. In order not to pay the premium costs of renting an existing shopping mall space, he decided to commission his own building.

Villa Moda is designed by Italian architect Pierfrancesco Cravel, with interiors by the British design firm Eldridge Smerin, and a brand identity created by Zurich- and London-based Wink Media. The building is a 9,300-square-metre (100,100-square-foot) glass cube emporium that overlooks the Persian Gulf. Inside the structure – a huge, four-way glass cube that resembles a giant, glass aquarium – each fashion label is given its own space and identity. Unusually, Villa Moda is the only civic building in Kuwait City that is not oriented towards Mecca. Instead, it is rotated a couple of degrees in order to afford the customers in the lounge the best view of the Gulf.

The building is set in a sculptural landscape that combines the simplicity of surface with the richness of layering and shadow, produced

1

2

1 Villa Moda resembles a transparent cube, surrounded by a slight frame of pillars.

2 With an identity by Wink Media, architecture by Pierfrancesco Cravel and interiors by Eldridge Smerin, Villa Moda is a hybrid between a commercial centre and a boutique.

3 The building itself is set in a sculptural landscape among 12-metre (39-foot) -high silver steel masts, designed to move with the wind and to light up at night, which surround the building.

93
VILLA MODA
PFC ARCHITECTS

by a field of 12-metre (39-foot) high silver, steel masts that surround the green glass envelope of the building. The slender masts, which have been designed to move with the wind, are illuminated with light-emitting diodes at the top. The theme is repeated with a radial veil of slender masts around the pale-coloured service elements at one end of the building and also in the new landscaped park between the building and the waterfront. Here the masts grow out of an irrigated green landscape, traversed by footpaths and sculptural elements that are visually ordered by the grid of the green building beyond.

Eldridge Smerin was commissioned to design the public areas – the Villa Moda Restaurant and lounge at the ground floor level, the Villa Moda Café on the first floor, overlooking the waterfront, and the two-level multibrand stores. They were briefed to deliver a concept that would capture the spirit of the location as well as producing a state-of-the-art retail environment. For the ground-floor restaurant, Eldridge Smerin designed a sculptural white structure within the single- and double-height volumes of the restaurant, thus creating a mix of small

and open dining areas. The enclosures are furnished with bespoke leather seating, while furniture by B&B Italia sits in the open spaces.

The multibrand space is defined by its dramatic rooflight that runs the full 30-metre (98-foot) length of the area. A parabolic diffuser, in which 320 cables are threaded, allows a changing installation of accessories and features. Other furniture by Verner Panton, Driade and Jasper Morrison for Cappellini complete this unique design-savvy take on the luxury bazaar.

4

5

6

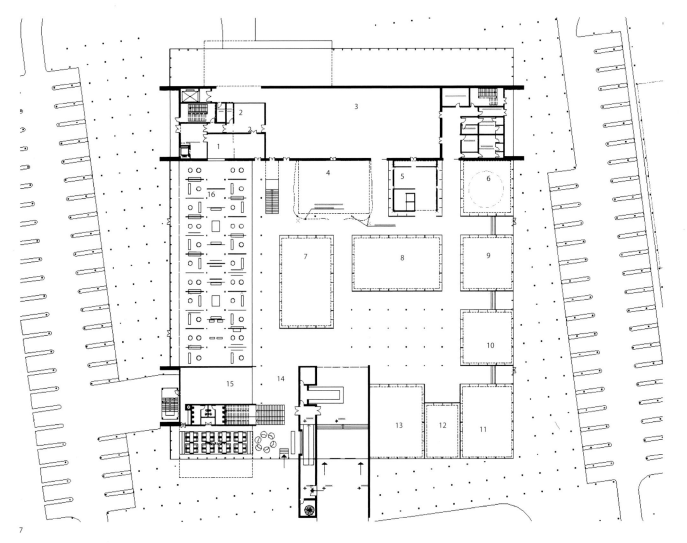

7

4 The multibrand space is defined by its dramatic rooflight that runs the full 30-metre (98-foot) length of the area.

5 The public areas, by Eldridge Smerin, are furnished with a mix of Driade, Cappellini and B&B Italia.

6 Within the building, each fashion brand has its own bespoke space.

7 Plan: 1. Taylor, 2. Depak Shop, 3. Warehouse, 4. Marni, 5. Miu Miu, 6. Etro, 7. Gucci, 8. Prada, 9. Prada Sport, 10. YSL, 11. Ferragamo, 12. B.V., 13. Fendi, 14. lounge, 15. kitchen, 16. multibrand warehouse.

Mandarina Duck's London 'destination' store, designed in 2002 by Dutch product designer Marcel Wanders, is intended to represent the specific values of the city. It features 40 breathing mannequins and a giant, seven-metre (23-foot) mannequin, inspired by *Gulliver's Travels*.

INTRODUCTION

In a bid to create an even more stimulating environment for design-savvy, but jaded, shoppers, retailers are increasingly collaborating with product and industrial designers to create concepts that stretch beyond the conventional, sleek, white-box format. Elements of subversion, irony or just an injection of a different perspective from that of architects, seem to have amazing results for some brands. Since 1998, Spanish interior and product designer Marti Guixé has 'overseen' the design of 13 shops around Europe for Camper, the Mallorcan brand that specializes in mid-priced Euro-funky shoes. For each shop, Guixé has developed a distinctive design, while maintaining the same visual language of humorous illustrations – part comic sketch, part user instructions, and part anti-materialistic slogan. The packaging reads, 'If you don't need it, don't buy it'. In 2004 Guixé helped Camper expand its brand with a FoodBALL shop in Barcelona, Spain. This health-food store/restaurant/take-away, also acts as a meeting point for the local community.

Similarly, Italian luggage and clothing brand Mandarina Duck approached Dutch design collective Droog Design to create its Paris store in 2000. Droog literally translates as 'dry wit', which sums up Droog's penchant for the amusing and humorous treatment of everyday objects, crafted with minimal simplicity as well as a careful choice of materials. Droog has made its name on the design scene for the way it has 'humanized' modern design, striking an emotional bond with enthusiasts. For the Paris store, architects Gijs Bakker and Renny Ramakers created a space filled with cocoon-like displays: brightly coloured bending structures that orbit around the rotating spiral staircase. Smaller items were hung on an inventive mutlicoloured rubber-band display system.

In 2002, Mandarina Duck repeated its strategy by commissioning Marcel Wanders to design its London Flagship store. Wanders, a product and furniture designer who has worked with top manufacturers like Cappellini and Flos, is also part of the Droog movement and with them shares the same quirky sense of humour.

INTERVIEW WITH MARCEL WANDERS OF MARCEL WANDERS STUDIO, AMSTERDAM, HOLLAND

You used a lot of irony in the Mandarina Shop in London, was that an attempt to provoke, stimulate, entertain or just a stylistic device?
'Part of the importance of designing Mandarina Duck for me was making sure that the customer loved it. It wasn't just about being featured in the press, but about creating a real experience. I based the design on myself, my needs – not only in terms of fun, but also looking exactly at how you would buy something. We created this idea of mannequins; they are usually boring to see, yet they are the best way to display the clothing, so I decided to create the most exciting mannequins ever. The result were breathing, bizarre yellow mannequins wearing clothes or just naked, but wearing a watch.'

Your background is largely product design – how do you think that informs the way you conceive a shopping experience?
'I think that what creative people are best at is to be generalist. Every time, we push to do things that we did not do before, and we make a new statement – every time. For me to design a shop was a completely different experience and I haven't done another since. On the product-development side, product designers have a tendency to work more on details – to be innovative on the small parts and make to sure they function. We look at an overall 3D plan that works in a functional and scale situation.'

What do you think of the 'patronage' between brands and designers or architects – Prada and Koolhaas, Marni and Future Systems, Pawson and Calvin Klein? Does it aim for a high profile, represent a modern-day version of a patron/artist relationship, or is it just a branding exercise?
'From a marketing point of view, designers are also now, more and more, a brand, so it's a two-way brand connection. The marketing side surely exists, but that's not the whole reason. I think collaboration between people who are honest can help both. We can also have fun doing it and it can be very simple. If we can create dreams, why change the winning team?'

How do you think retail design is changing?
'People in the world should be more fun and less boring. The good thing about design now is that stuff is getting less and less functional. And that's not only in retail. Functionality was so important for so many years after the Bauhaus movement, but functionality only counts for stuff we don't have to think about. I think there is a new movement in design that is changing perceptions and that considers the poetic side of things to be more important. The retail world is the perfect example. I was in Rockefeller Square, New York the other day and I just thought, "Even if I had no money in the world I would love to be here – you see so much more beauty, it's such a spectacle". Everybody in this world works to make a buck, but there is also the fun and the visual element to consider.'

Spanish designer Marti Guixé employs his trademark anarchic humour throughout the shops he has conceived for Camper. His collaboration with the Spanish footwear brand started in 1998 and has so far produced 13 shops, each designed to take account of the specific characteristics of the city they are in, while promoting the brand's spirit.

For the rolling-out of the Camper shops across the world, Guixé attempts to go beyond the idea of décor, using the presentation of shoes as a way in which to create a series of installations based on the information and the message.

The wordplay contained in Camper's slogan 'Walk in Progress' hints at 'work in progress'. It allows each shop to distance itself from the globalized standardization of many rollouts through an ever-changing product presentation, lighting, in-store graphics and photography.

For most of the Camper shops, Guixé plays with the notion of information design as an inexpensive form of decoration. The walls of the Barcelona shop (1998) are, for example, plastered with photographs, while the New York, SoHo shop (2000) is decorated with hand-drawn text. 'Camper is well-known for its graphic production, which appears on posters, bags and other publications. The idea of the info-shops is to take these characteristics to an extreme, bringing them all together to create a new typology of shop, based on the concept of information as decoration and decoration as information,' says Guixé.

1

2

The Munich Camper shop stands in an unusual location, an open triangle of space on the edge of the Fünf Höfe Building, designed by architects Herzog & de Meuron. The idea was to turn it into a 'meeting point': Camper shop, somewhere that shoppers could arrive when they were coming from Ludwigstrasse on their way toward the centre. To aid this 'meeting action', Guixé created a strong graphic device, a geometrical, bright-red façade that works for visual identification as well as being a reference to the Bavarian flag. 'The "Camper obstruction marking pattern" also acts as an attraction device: from very far away you see the pattern and that makes you go there. There is a space in between that you cannot identify, and once you are close you see perfectly the interior of the shop, as the squares are big enough. The effect is a kind of "curiosity generator"', says Guixé. Inside, carefully stacked rows of Camper shoes sit underneath the big industrial-looking lights by Ingo Maurer.

3

1 Low-cost, simple display systems allow for easy access to the merchandise, seen here in the Barcelona shop.

2 The red squares on the window display attract customers and are large enough to allow a glimpse of the inside.

3 The store's façade is a bright-red, graphic reference to the Bavarian flag.

More of a concept than a conventional shop, BLESS owes much to a type of retailing spearheaded by Colette, the *über* cool Paris shop that combines cutting-edge fashion, lifestyle and art installations. Indeed, the owners, Desiree Heiss and Ines Kaag, are fashion designers whose early careers were endorsed by Colette. Named after a bakery in a Berlin suburb, the BLESS duo excels at making unexpected juxtapositions and undermining expectations. For example, a DIY trainer kit, made of two New Balance soles, some fabric and instructions for combining the elements, as well as fur wigs made for the designer Martin Margiela, are just some of the duo's creations.

Initiated and created by long-term BLESS supporter and collector, Yasmine Gauster, one of the reasons to open a BLESS shop was the necessity to display, as completely as possible, the whole BLESS product and project range, which would have been difficult in a multibrand shop. It is of no coincidence that the BLESS 'flagship' store is in Berlin, a city that currently seems awash with unconventional retail formats, from the guerrilla shops of Comme des Garçons to low-budget, design-savvy sites.

Another reason to build the shop was to give the itinerant project 'BLESS N°11 BLESS shops' a temporary home. As a reaction to numerous invitations to art and design shows, often curated with a lot of enthusiasm

1, 2, 3 Innovative 'perpetual home motion machines' incorporate storage furniture and moving display.

4

5

3

4 The interior of the shop is constantly changing, sometimes decorated with plants and at other times with the merchandise.

5 In the summer, the shop expands temporarily into the outdoor space on the street or into a garden café.

6

6 BLESS shops are conceived to display merchandise
as well as art pieces that change constantly.

7

8

but small budgets, in 2000 BLESS came up with the idea of a temporary BLESS shop concept, adapting each time to local room situations and circumstances. The shop sales income manages to cover most of the shipping costs, enabling them to show a whole retrospective of the existing BLESS items. Temporary BLESS shops have opened in Basel, Stockholm, Zurich, Glasgow and Paris, among many others.

According to Desiree Heiss, 'So far, each BLESS shop has come out differently. One of the most interesting BLESS shops was during the Art Biennial in Werkleitz, which is in a region with very high unemployment. We didn't think there was any point in doing a shop, because there wasn't enough demand. So instead of opening a shop space, we looked for local stores that would host different products. The furniture shop had the chairware, the fashion shop had the scarves, and the hairbrush was in the hair salon. Of course, we didn't sell anything. The most abstract piece, The Set, was in the gas station.'

The Berlin location was conceived by Gauster, who has turned it into a main destination stop for BLESS fans. The shop's interior is constantly changing: sometimes its decorated with overgrown plants, other times it's emptied and populated only by BLESS N°22 perpetual home motion machines or used as a tearoom for restless Berlin fashion guests, etc. The dimensions are variable, as one of the main qualities of this concept is the space's flexibility. In the summer the shop can expand temporarily if desired, into the open space next to it, arranging itself as a garden café. It also sometimes crosses to the other side of the street, mixing with other designer's clothes in a multibrand store, or to temporarily occupy other empty locations in the same street.

7 Designed as a space to peruse, purchase or simply to have tea, BLESS shops are based on the idea of flexibility.

8 The BLESS shop was created to display the entire product and project range, something that would have been impossible in a multibrand shop.

1

1 The Barcelona store is designed as an organic space with curved walls, sculptured counters and bright-yellow colours.

2 The shiny buttercup-yellow epoxy floors contrast well with the cement columns.

3 From top: upper- and lower-level plans.

The Miss Sixty brand is the brainchild of Wicky Hassan, the energetic Italian entrepreneur and designer who is also behind the casual menswear label, Energie. Established 20 years ago in Italy, Miss Sixty is fast becoming something of a cult label among young fashionistas and models around the world. This is, no doubt, due to its eclectic selection of natty, vintage-like accessories and perfectly slim-fit jeans and trousers.

Like the collection, the look of the Miss Sixty shops is a careful mix of old and new, with glossy bespoke interiors creating a backdrop for modern period furniture pieces. The historical reference to the 1970s is carried out in the design with shiny surfaces, heavy velvet drapes in rich, saturated colours, and accent lighting, devised to create a warm and feminine atmosphere. The overall look is almost one of a thrift shop, an ironic, hyper-modernist pastiche aimed at the younger, style-conscious generations. Even if the clientele is too young to understand the cultural reference directly, the reference is widely accepted into their culture and is recognizable in the ambience it generates – it communicates an identity of place.

Florence-based Studio 63 Architecture and Design has been commissioned to design all 60 of the new Miss Sixty shops worldwide, of which three opened in the USA in 2003 – Los Angeles, San Francisco and Chicago. The Barcelona site was part of the new roll-out concept. An organic space, designed with curved walls, sculptured counters and

2

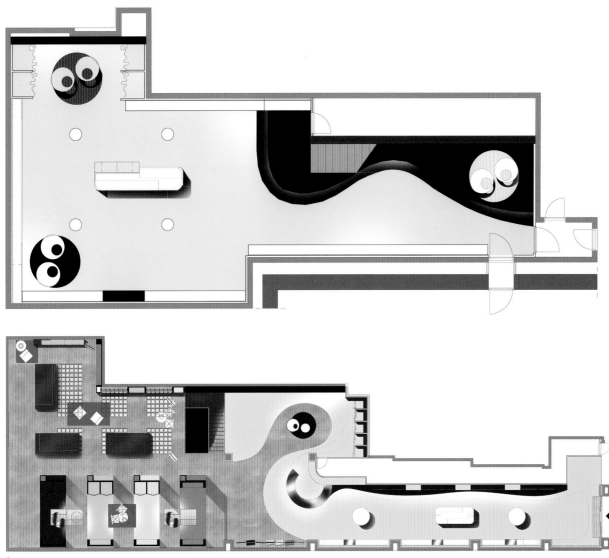

3

soft, cosy surfaces with bright colours is the leitmotif of all the stores worldwide. Each site is also individually conceived to retain the specific characteristics relating to its structure and location.

The Barcelona store features both the Miss Sixty and the Energie lines. Marco Zanuso's Lady chairs sit alongside more obscure 1970s pieces, while the sunny nature of Barcelona is reflected through the choice of bright colours and tones. Graphic design from the 1970s, the performance of David Bowie and the works of Verner Panton are all quoted as references.

4

5

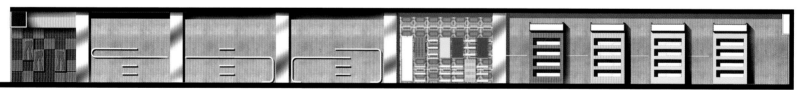

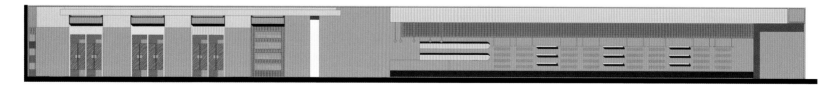

6

4 Lady chairs by Marco Zanuso add a retro feel to the store.

6 Internal elevations illustrate varying types of wall display.

5 Inspiration from the 1970s can be found in the velvet drapes that hang in the changing rooms, accent lighting and vintage furniture.

7 The in-built display shelves are lined with 1970s patterned wallpaper to enhance the retro feel.

7

A strong element of play is arguably one of the defining traits of Mandarina Duck's London 'destination' store, designed in 2002 by Dutch product designer Marcel Wanders. An upmarket, Italian luggage brand, Mandarina Duck has, over the years, created a niche for itself thanks to vividly coloured ranges, wear- and tear-resistant materials and youthful designs of bags and clothing. The collaboration between the company and Marcel Wanders started with the Murano bag collection and then developed with the commission of the London site.

Mandarina Duck calls its shops 'embassies'; each one is conceived to promote the culture of the city in which it is located. With its focus on bags, Mandarina Duck is a company for travellers and therefore the London site was conceived as a shop for international travellers. As part of this 'cultural relativist' approach to retail, the London site was intended to represent the specific values of the city, making it an exciting and desirable destination for discerning shoppers. 'In each city, the brand has some normal Mandarina shops and some very special sites,' explains Wanders. 'They need to be totally special and different from each other; they need to be interesting for a traveller since this is a brand devoted to them.'

The London store was conceived as a place to be experienced – where the atmosphere is changing constantly. In Wanders' words, the shop should be 'not only a place where you buy clothes and bags, but also a store that will sell and hand you over the secrets of the city'.

Design-wise, the concept was initially devised for the Rome site and then moved to London. The underlying idea was that it would be a fun and living place to make purchases. Bathed in the brand's yellow trademark colour, the shop is defined by the presence of 40 bizarre, breathing mannequins that display the brand's clothing and accessories.

2

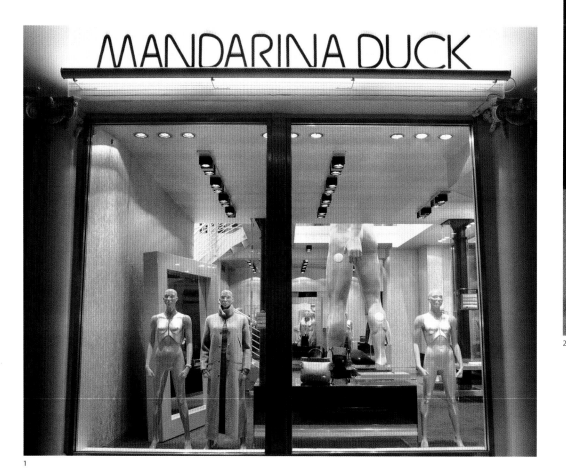

1

1 The central area of the shop is defined by a giant, yellow mannequin that was inspired by *Gulliver's Travels* and contains an audio system.

2 The store has a double-height ceiling space, no internal walls and a large, swirling silver staircase.

Inside, the construction was overseen by architects Harper MacKay, although it was Wanders' idea to knock down all the internal walls and create a double-height space. The central area is defined by a large, open space filled with a giant seven-metre (23-foot) mannequin, inspired by the giants in *Gulliver's Travels* and with a torso containing an audio system. This archetypical British traveller, Gulliver, lives in the store that is appropriately renamed WanderDuck.

In the middle of the shop is also a swirling silver staircase, around which a large, chromed, two-floor-high wall breathes and changes its surface from convex to concave in a constant fluid rhythm. Outside the building, a fairy-tale-like stream of bubbles float onto the pavement to further amplify the metaphor of a breathing, living building.

The building of the store generated a huge amount of press coverage, reinforcing the notion that often the effect of an imaginative retail design is stronger than any high-profile advertising campaign. For Wanders, the celebration of local culture not only guarantees that customers get more than what they bargained for, but that they will also return. Creating a space that provokes an emotional response, a spectacle rather than a functional environment, was the final effect the Dutch designer was after.

3

4

5

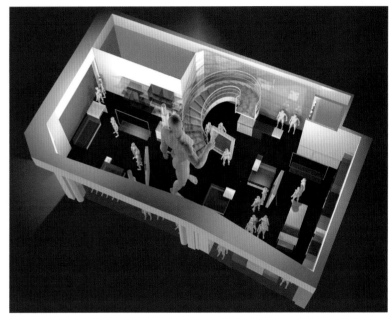

3 The large, chromed, double-floor-high wall breathes by changing its surface from convex to concave in a constant fluid rhythm.

4 Luggage, accessories and the clothing line are displayed in glass cabinets or on the yellow mannequins.

5 Computer renderings of the upper and lower levels of the London Mandarina Duck store.

Apple's retail location in the Ginza district of Tokyo allows visitors access to the latest Apple products and aims to promote a stylish, technology-filled lifestyle. The simple and minimal furniture gives emphasis to the elegant computer hardware that is on display.

pro

pro

Someone you know would love a PowerBook.

The 17-inch PowerBook.

INTRODUCTION

From airports to railway stations, trade fair exhibition stands to hypermarkets, retail possibilities are proliferating in new ways and in unexpected spaces. Part transit, part mall and part theatre space, these post-Modern locations offer exciting challenges for designers. As traditional new location opportunities thin out and ground rents become prohibitively high, retailers are rethinking ways to attract customers with new format strategies. Crucial retail analysis, by brand strategy and design group Lippincott Mercer, discusses the importance of tailoring the offer to the customers' differing mindsets.

From food to financial services and interiors, choice depends not just on a customer's demographic profile, but on what mindset they are in. This may be determined by factors such as the time of day, what they happen to be doing at the time or where they are located. So, while a customer might just want a lunchtime sandwich at the railway station branch of a grocery outlet, a substantial weekly shop would only be contemplated at a larger branch somewhere else. Any local bank might be the perfect place to collect some cash, but at other times it can also be the place to acquire critical, life-changing services, such as a mortgage. Similarly, furnishing and interior stores may serve as 'giftware' stores at the same time as catering for both long-term acquisition purchases as well as off-the-shelf 'quick-buy' purchases.

In technology, for example, as the use of mobile phones reaches saturation point, telecoms companies have had to create new strategies to attract customers. Rather than just selling them a new handset and network deals, Orange stores now offer a whole wide range of accessories and customer services that reinforce brand values and insure loyalty. The new spate of Apple stores, which have recently opened worldwide, allow Apple to take control of the sales experience and align it with its well-conceived brand values of functional restraint and beautiful design. Here the sales desks are hidden and the covetable products placed in full view for everyone to touch and buy off the shelf. Defined by German design group Dan Pearlman as 'brand architecture', this staging of retail experiences sees retail design and architecture as just one element of the overall brand strategy.

INTERVIEW WITH VOLKER KATSCHINSKI OF DAN PEARLMAN, BERLIN, GERMANY

Can you define brand architecture?
'Brands are the result of countless sensual impressions and experiences. Brand architecture means creating worlds in which all perceived elements become fused into an emotional experience. The benefits of architecture and communication are combined to develop solutions for 3D brand management. Forms, colours, materials, sounds and scents turn the brand into an authentic experience for all the senses. At exhibitions or events, in stores or clubs, the atmosphere and dramaturgy of a brand integrates the visitors and makes them part of a unique experience.'

How does brand architecture need to work differently compared to, say, traditional retail environments?
'The fundamental idea of brand architecture is to stage shopping experiences and to provide a platform for the products. People want more than a product. They want stories – experiences – and they want to react to this in a physical and emotional way. A shop is not a mere PoS (point of sale) but a PoC (point of contact): normally a brand tries to make a promise, but with brand architecture the brand has to keep and prove this promise. The visitor gets directly in touch with the brand; he learns about its context and personality. If the visitor can identify with these brand values, the brand seems sympathetic to him and he buys the products.'

How important is the emotional element in the architecture? How do you define experience?
'The emotional aspect is very important. Nowadays, design is focused on an experience for all senses, therefore brand architecture is visually spectacular, integrates scents and arouses emotions. Products and brands create experiences through haptic (physical feedback) elements or applied materials. The more senses that are activated, the more comprehensive the total brand experience is. It is a matter of the idea of sustainability in self-contained atmospheres. People want experiences – TV, cinema; each experience and emotion is reproduced. This need for experience leads to the staging of experiences. The importance lies in the emotional accessibility of a brand. Brand architecture does not only mirror the brand, but becomes a "point of me". Individuals are incorporated through scents, sounds, forms, materials, colours and light. All of which are very emotional elements in architecture.'

You have worked for car manufacturer Audi, fashion brand Escada and telecoms company O$_2$. Are these the types of products that are better represented by brand architecture?
'Our clients belong to the areas of automobiles, telecommunication, lifestyle and fashion: products that are strongly brand-associated; premium products in contrast to mass-consumer goods.'

We are seeing an increase of 'alternative' spaces for shopping, from airports, to stations, vending machines, trade fairs. What is their attraction and function? Do you see the future of retail moving in that direction?
'Ever since the age of the Internet, consumption takes place not only in shops but everywhere and all the time. New selling channels constantly come along. Eventually every brand has to decide for itself, whether these new vending channels make sense or not for their brand or products.'

Brand roll-outs need to take into account the specific locality and cultural differences of consumers across the world. How do you take these elements into account in your work?
'The differentiation depends on the brand. For example, BMW emphasizes its consistent worldwide branding, but to avoid a "culture-clash", every country has its own focal point. Puma and MINI emphasize their internationality, with the effect that they communicate their brand at different places with different means. The specific "genius loci" of a city/country is included in the respective brand appearance.'

In the digital age, how important do you think the physical experience of shopping is, and why?
'The physical experience of shopping remains very important. The Internet, which can be seen as an example of the digital age, is a new medium, but it is complementary to traditional media (just like television has not displaced theatre or cinema yet). But when we are shopping, nothing can replace the feeling of holding a product in your own hands. This is especially important when buying products like shoes or clothes. Other factors that customers search for during shopping are distraction, change and entertainment. These feelings cannot be replaced, either.'

Retail design is often conceived together with brand strategy, and nowhere is this more evident than in retail environments for telecoms brands. Risking easy consumption-saturation levels, they have to find new ways in which to attract consumer spending power. The challenge for the design team developing a new store environment for Orange was how to combine sector-leading communications technology with a 'human' face that would encourage customers to visit. By providing 'the best experience of Orange for the customer', the aim was to become the first and last stop for customers, encouraging higher visit frequency, dwell-time and conversion rates. The idea was to provide a sensory experience that would show that everyday technology can also be fun.

The design team, led by Simon Stacey, then creative director at 20/20 in London, and now partner at Lippincott Mercer, addressed the

1

2

needs of the two distinct customer types: the 'fast', time-pressured, mission-driven shopper, and the 'slow', browsing shopper. The store design has three major elements – shop, recharge and play – that all meet the different shopping behaviours of these two groups of customers.

The 'shop' element is the area where customers can browse the ranges of mobile phones, encouraged to interact with the open-floor orange 'merchandising cubes' where the tactility of the phones is reinforced by the tactility of the coloured foam display-pads. Customers shopping in this area have a dedicated service desk where they are encouraged to 'fall in love' with the products as well as the brand.

The 'recharge' element is an in-store zone where time-pressured customers are offered the appropriate mobile service, quickly and efficiently, at a dedicated 'time is precious' service desk. In this area there is also a self-service wall where customers can recharge their phones and top-up their cards. For those customers who have urgent problems that

1 Merchandising cubes reinforce the tactility of the browsing experience through coloured foam display-pads.

2 Customers visiting the 'shop' area have a dedicated service desk where they can engage with the products as well as the brand.

3

need resolving, there is a 'we're all ears' service desk, specifically for problem solving. All the service desks are highlighted by over-scaled graphic walls, using 3D icons such as hearts, clocks and ears that communicate the service quickly and with a humour that conveys the human dimension of Orange.

The third element, 'play', is key to bringing an exciting experiential dimension to the store, as well as encouraging customers to return to Orange. The 'play' areas allow customers to interact with and learn more about Orange, while browsing the store. All of the phones on the 'merchandising cubes' are live and allow customers to play with and test the product, on their own or with Orange 'phone trainers'. In the centre of the store is the 'play table' – an interactive console where up to four players can engage in digital games that also reveal information on mobile phone content. Above the play table is a large projection cube where moving images and sound provide animation across the store.

At the back of the store are the 'terraces' – a series of rising platforms containing interactive 'pods' where customers can compose and download their own ringtones, as well as create and download screen designs for their mobile phones. The terraces also provide seating to watch the animation, have consultations with phone trainers, or to meet friends. The final social element is where customers can try out the phones, take photos with them and then stick their photos and messages onto a giant Orange logo on the back wall.

3 On the large back wall, at the top of the terraces, customers can try out the phones, take photos and stick them onto the Orange logo.

4 All the service desks are characterized by over-scaled graphic walls using 3D icons such as ears that communicate the service quickly and with humour.

For this flagship store, German design group Dan Pearlman translated the brand values of telecoms company O_2 into a 3D interactive space. Conceived to represent a brand experience, rather than just a selling point, the main architectural focus is given by the central 'interactive media band'. This starts on the outer façade with a 3D O_2 logo, then runs across the ceiling and floor inside the shop. The content of the band can be changed according to the seasons and store's needs – for the opening it was set up to evoke a winter mood. When a visitor steps onto the surface of the band, cracks and splits appear on the projected ice surface.

The band runs through the shop and leads into a table area where products, information and prices hover through the ice. When the visitor touches an object, the text or product information fades at the point of touch. On the rear wall, the media band shows excerpts of current O_2 television commercials with testimonials in real-life size or 360-degree product demonstration films. The colour scheme of the store also reiterates the winter, crisp mood with white displays and blue lighting.

1 The side of the façade features the O_2 logo and stations for topping up phone cards.

2 A band that starts on the outer façade and unfolds into the store represents O_2's brand.

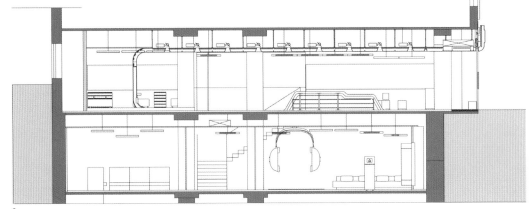

4

5

6

3 Long section through the ground and basement levels. The entrance is top right.

4 In-store graphics illustrate the changing seasons, while custom-made display units make the products easily accessible to customers.

5 Giant earphones act as a playful, decorative device.

6 The products are displayed in a way that allows customers to touch them and try them out.

Another strong, eye-catching element is represented by the Top 10 conveyor belt displayed in the front window. The belt carries ten transparent containers with O_2 products and detailed information about them. A touch-sensitive area on the window glass allows the information to be paused and read through. Interactive exhibits in the store, such as 'Photopoint' and 'Interactive Island' invite the visitor to take time to touch them and try them out, offering intuitive and playful insights. Dan Pearlman intends the store design to be an energetic and fresh format that reflects the brand's communication ethos and offers an island for customers, 'entirely geared towards their individual needs'.

7

9

7 Seating and accessible touch points invite customers to try out the O_2 services.

8 From left: basement and ground-floor plans.

9 For the opening of the store, the band was set up to evoke a winter mood with cracks and splits projected onto it to represent an icy surface.

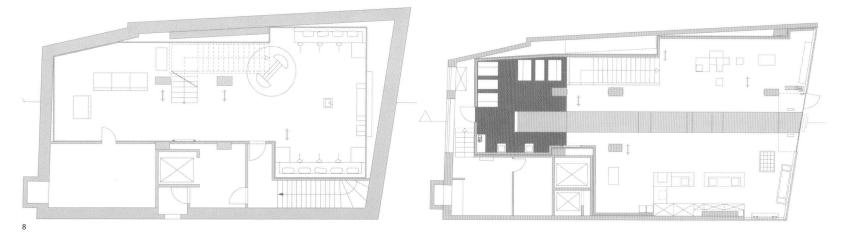

1

Since Apple Computers Inc. opened its first retail store in America in May 2001, 70 more, visited by over 24 million visitors, have followed in the USA alone. The 'hands-on Apple Store experience' allows visitors access to the latest Mac computer systems and digital lifestyle applications, including the iconic iPod. All Apple Stores come equipped with an eight-metre (27-foot) long Genius Bar, one of the most popular sections of the Apple retail stores, where visitors can ask a 'Mac Genius' questions or receive product service. In the Internet café, anyone can check e-mail or use Apple's iChat AV and iSight, and customer events every month include a Studio Series of hands-on training classes.

Apple Computer's retail location opened in the Ginza district of Tokyo in 2004. The retail environment aims to replicate the company's success in promoting a stylish, technology-filled lifestyle, with simplicity and efficiency. Like so many buildings in Tokyo, the Ginza store has a vertical orientation. An eight-storey building, it has been renovated by Bohlin Cywinski Jackson into a simple rectilinear form. The façade uses bead-blasted stainless-steel panels at the first three levels, which is where the Apple logo is minimally displayed. The remaining five floors use an

2

3

1 An eight-storey building, the Ginza store's façade is composed of steel and laminated glass panels.

2 The first three floors of the façade, where the Apple logo is displayed, uses bead-blasted, stainless-steel panels.

3 Apple products sit on minimally designed maple tables while the elevators at the end ensure the visitors' flow is extended to the upper floors.

4

5

6

4 Grey limestone and bead-blasted stainless steel on the walls and floors, as well as simple maple tables, are used.

5 Internet stations are kept minimally furnished to give emphasis to the computers and software.

6 The 84-seat, state-of-the-art theatre is used for lectures and presentations.

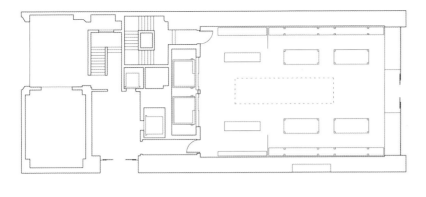

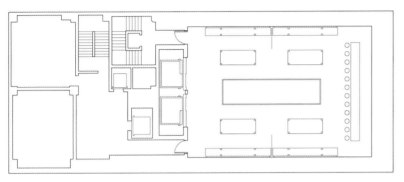

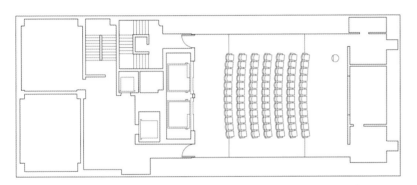

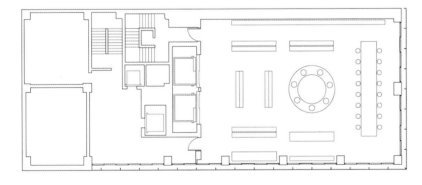

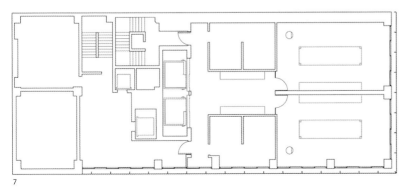

open-joint glass rain-screen system in front of floor-to-ceiling stainless-steel sliding glass doors. The double skin employs ceramic-fitted, laminated glass panels with a special interlayer, creating a minimal, elegant external curtain that provides thermal protection to the internal second skin.

To overcome the vertical structure and to make sure the visitor's flow is uninterrupted, Apple conceived custom-designed, all-glass elevators to create a seamless shopping experience. The elevators were built as transparent as possible, using Otis all-glass doors that require no frames and with the shaft of the elevator exposed to full view behind a large expanse of clear glass. The two cabs operate as shuffle cars rather than traditional elevator cars, which means that the rider does not call the lift, but rather enters the car when it rolls past and is taken automatically to the next floor. The cabs are synchronized to move in opposite directions, passing each other in the middle of the shaft. This stratagem allows for the elevators to feel like a continuation of the shop's space or a sort of vertical moving walkway connecting all five floors.

The five floors offer various ways to experience the Apple product line, from casual browsing on the shop floors to active learning in the studio classrooms or the 84-seat, state-of-the-art theatre. Throughout different levels, grey limestone and bead-blasted stainless steel are used on the floors and the walls. The furniture in the store comprises simply detailed maple tables and benches, minimally arranged to give emphasis to the elegant computers and software on display. Customers can look and touch the products on display, then order and purchase them at the till counter. On the store's third and fifth levels, grey acoustical fabric walls and carpets, coupled with luxurious seating, set the tone for the learning environment of the theatre and demonstration classrooms.

7 From top: plans of the ground through fourth floors.
The entrance is to the right of the ground-floor plan.

7

Italian furniture manufacturer B&B Italia, commissioned architects John Pawson and Antonio Citterio for their first flagship store in London. Formerly a car showroom, the airy interiors, designed by Citterio, are bathed in natural light from oversized windows and skylights.

INTRODUCTION

In using 'lifestyle', retailers don't just want to sell goods, they want consumers to aspire to a brand as a promise of a way of living. Those retailers that have not so far used lifestyle are gradually realizing it as a means of expanding their range of goods. Fashion brands such as Donna Karan, Armani and Fendi have all jumped on the lifestyle bandwagon, producing their own range of furniture, while the lifestyle champ, Ikea, with its cheap prices and clean design, seems to have conquered almost every corner of Europe, if not the Western world. Vittorio Radice, then executive director of the new Marks & Spencer 'Home' business, made the groundbreaking decision of commissioning minimalist architect John Pawson to create a 'house structure' for Marks and Spencer's innovative 2004 Lifestore building in Gateshead, UK. While the architectural pedigree was excellent, the concept failed to gel with Marks & Spencer's rather disappointing homeware collection.

Perhaps the most interesting novelty is this area was the rise of the concept store in the 1990s. Shops like Colette in Paris, Corso Como in Milan and TAD Conceptstore in Rome are a reflection of the personality of the owners and their editing capacities, not just the brands they sell. Here, what is being proposed is an idealized, holistic lifestyle concept, comprised of clothes and also magazines, flowers, perfumes, homeware and even their own compilation CDs, edited in the same way as the merchandise.

The notion that retail could offer a lifestyle experience arguably started in 1964 with Habitat's first outlet in London. Here, for the first time, customers could pick and choose furniture to create an environment that was reflective of the 1960s' joyous mode of living and that was counterbalanced by informed, modern design. The shop was a huge success in London; John Lennon, George Harrison and film stars like Julie Christie all bought furniture there.

Habitat was, of course, the brainchild of Sir Terence Conran, who went on to build an empire based on retail, restaurants and redevelopment. Habitat was the first shop to identify its products and its image as part of a wider ethos. Its groundbreaking idea was to offer a stylish, affordable way of living to the masses, while introducing products like the chicken brick or the duvet – a reflection of Conran's admiration for Continental ways of living. During the 1970s' Conran went on to open international chains of Habitat stores and The Conran Shop. Today he is still the owner of the The Conran Shop, with stores around the world.

INTERVIEW WITH SIR TERENCE CONRAN OF CONRAN & PARTNERS, LONDON, UK

How has the shopping experience changed from when you started in the UK in the 1960s?

'In the 1960s, stores looked like dreary warehouses. There were rows of stock, all pushed far too close, and bad lighting. There was nothing in it that made it a pleasurable experience. We must remember that we had just come out from an era of rationing, and things had been in short supply. There was no reason why a retailer should make a particular effort, since the shopping experience was driven by needs rather than wants. The real revolution was when retailers discovered that they could create a brand out of the product. As a consequence, the brand became something special and shopping stopped being this endless discounting experience. When we started Habitat, we were also running Mothercare and Next. We soon realized that if we designed the product ourselves, and branded it, we would create a reason to go to our shops. By creating your own brand, which sold at a lower price, you build a house brand and build the loyalty of customers.'

How do you feel Habitat influenced UK shopping and living patterns?

'Habitat was the first lifestyle store. The stores at that time, certainly in the furnishing area, were unfocused, and that was the reason I started Habitat, since I was making furniture and used to get depressed about the totally untargeted selection of merchandise that you found in the stores. I wanted to sell furniture in an environment that was surrounded by a collection that had a point of view. With Habitat I soon realized that if you create a busy store, it becomes a successful store. For example, we were the first to put cafés in shops so the customers could sit down and talk and think. If you want an atmosphere, create an energetic place where visitors feel part of a club. The Habitat philosophy was that you took the thing off the shelf yourself, like a supermarket, and unlike other shops you didn't really have to have an interaction with a salesperson.'

You own and have designed both shops and restaurants. For both of them you emphasize the need to create a 'busy', theatrical experience. What's the difference between retail and leisure?

'The restaurant is really a form of the shop of the future. There is an open kitchen, where you can see everything being made and an incredible busy energy. But also in retail, for example, you can have a manufacturer of glass in the shop showing off his skills or a clothes-alteration service.

It creates a spectacle, and it gets rid of the static quality that you see in many shops. Supermarkets are increasingly doing it: for example, by cooking bread on the premises. In Milan, for example, there is a fantastic shop where a guy is cracking Parmesan on a table and there is always a queue of people behind it. That sticks in my memory and I know I will get the best possible cheese and not something old wrapped in clingfilm. It's a ritual and a spectacle, and the only way for smaller shops to survive is to offer something different, a particular service, and to elevate the experience.'

How has the customer changed in the past years? Are they completely jaded or can you still offer possible visions of living?

'Yes, I think you can. Big chains are producing things that are very pleasant. Certainly there is now a huge offer in the high street. When we started Habitat, many were skeptical about it working outside the capital. But we prepared the ground by sending out catalogues in the other parts of the country and then, when we eventually opened a shop there, we had already created demand. I believe that people can't buy what is not offered, so what really informs people's tastes is what the shops offer. And the merchandise is your best message.'

Zurich-based architects Brunner Eisenhut Gisi were commissioned to design a new food hall concept in 2001. Globus Food Hall proposes itself as a 'house of food', a glamorous food emporium where shoppers can enjoy a total food experience – roaming through the delicatessen, the bar/take away and the kitchen and table department. Architecturally, the store is divided into three separate floors over a space of 2,125 square metres (22,870 square feet).

The basement floor delicatessen attempts to replicate the feel of an open-air fruit and vegetable market. The areas are divided into a room for fruit and vegetables, another for perishable goods and a third for the cash till and customer service. A fourth room displays an impressive selection of wines.

Cold-cuts of meat, prepared salads, smoked fish, seafood and shellfish, charcuterie, cheese, chocolates, spices, bottled and packaged foods and imported fruit are displayed in an accessible way, either perched on tables or behind counters.

1

2

1 Globus Food Hall is a light and airy store, divided over three separate floors.

2 The take-away area is at the heart of the ground floor, which is also home to the flower shop, homeware and the gift section.

3

4

3 Customers can savour produce from the delicatessen at informal, high-counter tables.

4 The take-away and florist sections are clearly visible through the store's glass façade.

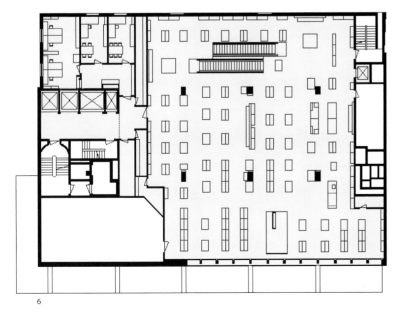

The Italian counter offers piles of fresh pasta in pretty pastel shades; marinated aubergines (eggplant), artichokes, and black, green and purplish olives piled on white dishes. The Japanese counter allows customers to watch a sushi chef slicing and rolling the pink fish and placing it carefully into the neat *bento* boxes. On the shelves are stacked fish sauce, sambal olek, glass noodles, egg noodles, basmati rice, pickled limes and tahini paste. Each shelf has a label to indicate where the food came from – India, Japan, China, even the UK. The aim is to replicate a neighborhood shop, with the familiarity and the customer service that comes with it. The basement atmosphere provides a cellar-like atmosphere, with an emphasis on the fresh and earthy qualities.

The take-away area is at the heart of the ground floor. It is a room with a high, transparent glass wall, which is used as a divider for the different sections that are designed as four big modules – panini/tapas, bar, wok and sushi. Cross-selling shelves across the membrane display the goods range of the delicatessen floor. High-counter tables with chairs allow customers to sit for informal self-service snacks. Sleekly and elegantly designed, the narrow dining tables come equipped with silverware, napkins, condiments and glasses, all ready and waiting for the customers. There's a wine and coffee bar if you want a special drink, and the food counters also dispense mineral water and other simple drinks. Next door are the flower shop, giftware and a very design-oriented home furnishing section, which continues onto the first upper floor and faces directly out onto the street outside.

5 In the basement, wooden floors and dark panelling convey a cellar-like atmosphere for the impressive selection of wines.

6 From top: plans of the lower basement (used for storage and refrigeration), upper basement (delicatessen) and first floor (household items).

6

1

1 The B&B Italia showroom is the result of a collaboration between John Pawson and Antonio Citterio.

2 Street elevation: the glass façade (centre right) sits in between existing older buildings.

3 Formerly a car showroom, the site is characterized by a striking façade of sheet glass, natural stone and bronze.

Italian furniture manufacturer B&B Italia decided to commission British architect John Pawson and Italian architect Antonio Citterio for its first flagship store in London. Founded in 1966 by the Busnelli family, B&B has always focused on contemporary furniture born out of an enlightened commissioning relationship with well-known designers. The decision to open a store in London was part of a larger trend that saw many Italian furniture companies such as Artemide and Driade open new concessions or flagship stores in international markets. In the bid for the discerning customer, London had emerged as a ripe market.

Both Pawson and Citterio had previously designed collections for the Italian company, so the project was built on an established working relationship, which benefited from shared values and an understanding of the company's vision. Citterio, in particular, had worked as a product designer and consultant for B&B for 30 years.

2

3

4

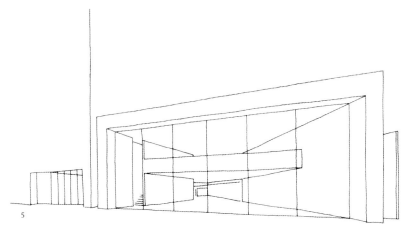

5

4 Inside, a large wooden staircase leads to the interiors by
Antonio Citterio. The long wall of the ground floor is
covered in grey slate tiles.

6

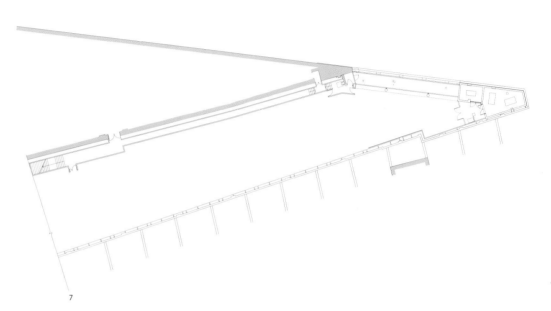

7

The site, which stretches more than 1,200 square metres (12,920 square feet) from the glamorous shops and Georgian villas of Brompton Cross in London to the more prosaic urban scenery of South Kensington's railway tracks, was formerly a car showroom. The striking façade, created by Pawson, is composed of sheet glass, natural stone and bronze. It appears from the street as a piece of monumental sculpture, one that is both grand yet restrained in its style. Inside, a large wooden ramp leads into the airy interiors created by Citterio. These are defined by oversized windows and skylights, which span the whole length of the building and bathe it in natural light. The long wall of the ground floor is covered in grey slate tiles.

A division of space that is created with the insertion of a mezzanine level defines the interior architecture. The mezzanine area is of white enameled steel, dark-grey ceilings and strong accent lighting. This space, with its reduced height, light wood flooring and decorative lighting fixtures, aims to recreate a landscape of domestic comfort, while maintaining an open proportion and fluid continuity of space,

and remaining open, overlooking the floor below. Pieces of furniture stand alone or are displayed in comfortable settings resembling real rooms. Unlike other furniture companies, B&B Italia does not propose a 'total living' concept but is more interested in emphasizing its product line. Furniture is not displayed as museum pieces, but is comfortably offset by Citterio's design. B&B Italia also has stand-alone showrooms in Italy, Germany and Japan.

5 Sketch of the glass façade.

6 In the mezzanine area, pieces of furniture stand alone or are displayed in comfortable settings like domestic rooms.

7 Plan: the street façade is shown top right, and the mezzanine top left.

7

1

1 Old and modern mix seamlessly as custom-made crystal display cabinets show off the Baccarat collection.

2 In this luxurious, decadent atmosphere, mirrors, crystal chandeliers and red tones are employed by Starck to give the space a theatrical air.

The allure of Baccarat's new headquarters in Paris relies on two major assets: the mercurial talents of prolific designer Philippe Starck and the history of its location. This aristocratic townhouse in the sixteenth *arrondissement* was, during the first half of the twentieth century, the home of the Viscountess Marie-Laure de Noailles – art patron, muse and financer of Surrealist 'oeuvres' such as Luis Buñuel's *L'Age d'Or* and Jean Cocteau's *Le Sang d'un Poete*. The viscountess also held memorable parties here, a careful mix of aristocrats and artists set against the backdrop of a cream shagreen and parchment-lined sitting room, designed by Jean Michel Frank.

Starck was given carte blanche to develop the Maison Baccarat headquarters, its boutique and gallery museum, a restaurant and showroom. Inspired by a place so laden with memories and by 'the world of illusion' that the luxury brand evokes, he designed a space filled with contrasts, opulence and modernity. Dadaist and Surrealist touches are a clever nod to the Maison's previous owners.

A crystal chandelier is plunged into a large glass aquarium at the entrance, a 2.4-metre (eight-foot) -tall mirror throne stands on the ground floor, while the hallway is lined with giant mirrors leading to a main staircase illuminated by fibre optics.

2

3

3 In the private dining room, furnished with pink fabric, a jet-black chandelier hangs in pride of place.

4

4 The 12.8-metre (42-foot) custom-made crystal table in the 'transparent' room is used to display glassware.

5

6

Baccarat was founded in 1764, thanks to a grant from the king of France, Louis XV. In just a few years Baccarat had established itself as the leading French crystal manufacturer and soon became the most prestigious in the world. The company, now owned by the Société du Louvre and backed by the Taittinger group, is well-known for its emphasis on techniques and creativity as well as the high standard of its glassblowers, cutters and engravers. More recently, the brand has diversified into luxury accessories and wristwatches.

Some of the most prestigious pieces from the Baccarat collection are housed in the gallery-museum. Crystal thrones created for Indian maharajas; the custom-ordered, monumental Tsar Nicholas II's candelabra; limited-edition collections by Georges Chevalier and Ettore

Sottsass, and dessert plates made for Coco Chanel, decorated with etchings of seamstress scissors. The Crystal Room Restaurant combines exposed brickwork with decadent baroque gilt frames, rooms of pink fabric and satin banquettes as well as bespoke furniture by Starck. In the private dining room a black crystal chandelier hangs in pride of place.

In this glamorous ambience, the shopping experience is elevated to a refined demonstration of discerning taste – a 12.8-metre (42-foot)-long crystal table, which can be custom-ordered at a smaller size, crystal chopsticks and candelabras are just some of the items on sale. The retail space here is conceived as a fluid concept, the focus being the historic narrative of the house and its extraordinary décor.

5 In the ground floor, the specially lit glass case contrasts with the beige concrete walls.

6 The stylized figures that support the glass display cabinets are Starck's subtle nod towards the surrealist past of the building.

8

7 The palatial staircase is illuminated by fibre optic lights.   8 Surrealist humour is displayed by Starck with the 2.4-metre (eight-foot)-high mirror throne that stands on the glass floor.

As much of a showroom as a store, the l.a.Eyeworks shop occupies an existing two-storey building on the corner of Martel and Beverly Boulevards in Los Angeles. Known for its angular frames, l.a.Eyeworks is a brand that has always promoted spectacles as fashion objects to complement a stylish lifestyle. Its advertising campaigns feature famous bespectacled faces along with the slogan: 'A face is like a work of art. It deserves a frame'. The company has always been keen to celebrate an alliance with creative fields through its window displays, website and advertising campaigns.

For the Beverly Boulevard store, l.a.Eyeworks asked Neil Denari to create a space that retained both the temporary qualities of a retail environment and the stability more conventionally associated with institutional or public buildings. Although not tied to a specific budget or brief, the client asked Denari to create a design that would hold up for a long time, not just a few years. While fashion is intentionally based on quick stylistic shifts, the client asked that the design of the store resist not the ephemeral nature of fashion, but rather the fashion of architecture without recurring to minimalism or lack of expression.

Denari tried to make the most of the corner site of the building. He left the upper part of the stucco façade intact, partly to comply with local building regulations. The two main functional requirements – a transparent front and that the products are visible and accessible to the customers – are solved with the use of a glazed front. This engages window-shoppers through the displays for which l.a.Eyeworks is renowned.

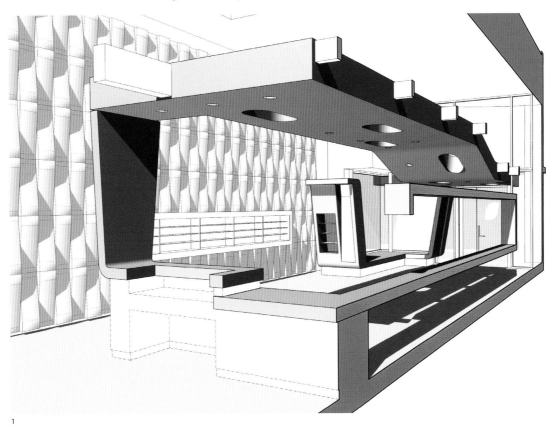

1

1 A computer rendering of the main internal display structure of the store.

2 Denari made the most out of the corner site of the building, leaving the stucco façade intact and creating a transparent frontage.

3 The glazed front engages window-shoppers with a selection of glasses displays.

4 Cutaway computer rendering shows how the display structure occupies the two-storey space.

2

3

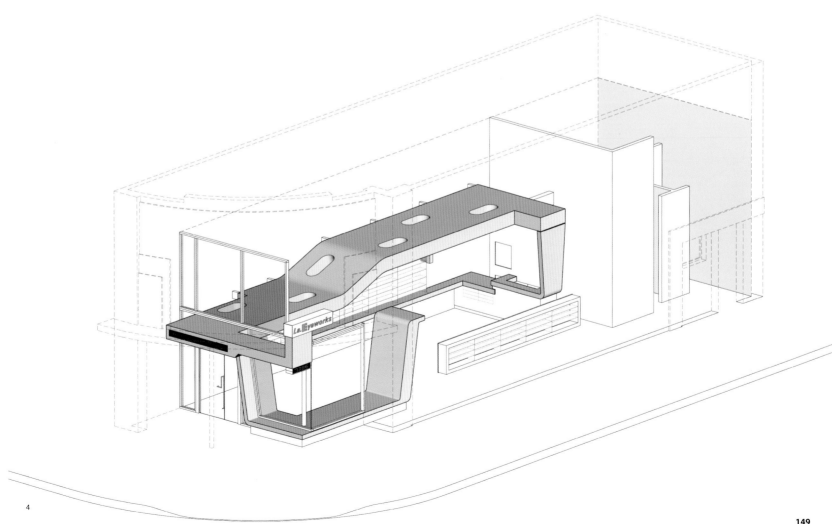

4

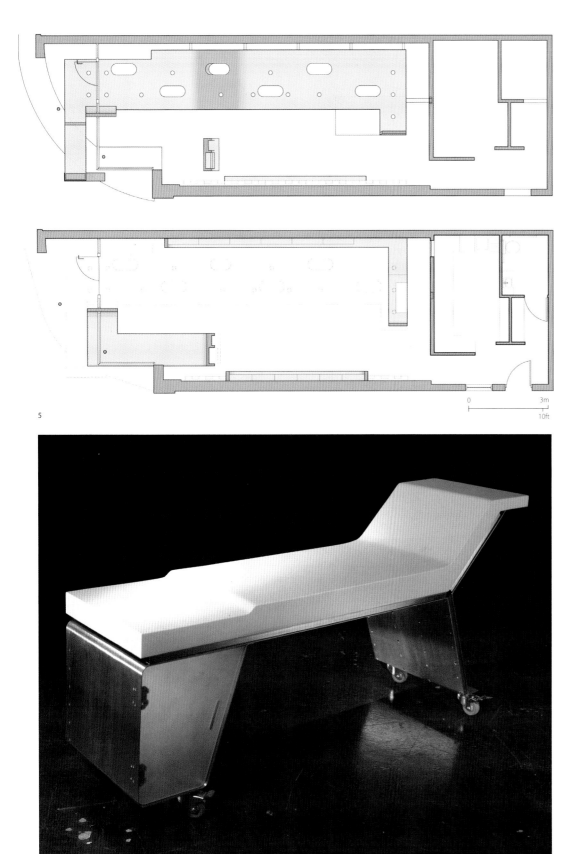

5 From top: plans of the top and bottom of the display structure show the layout of the store.

6 Furniture on wheels by NMDA functions as both benches and shelving units.

7 The blue epoxy terrazzo floor matches the shop fitting elements, and a wall of vacuum-formed panels serves as an installation by Jim Isermann.

Inside, a gaseous blue surface unwinds itself like a ribbon through the store to perform many functions: window display, bench, shelving unit and sales counter. LED screens embedded into the edge of the blue slab flash advertising slogans and news to passing pedestrians and drivers. In between the merchandise and the blue slab are a series of blue-tinted furniture elements, such as shelving structures, designed by NMDA. The epoxy polymer-based terrazzo floor is painted ocean blue to match the furniture and shop-fitting elements. On one side, a wall of vacuum-formed panels, an installation designed by Jim Isermann, fills the entire west wall of the store. The piece acts as a thick, 2D vertical surface where the repetitive pattern of the panels forms a graphic field against which the rest of the store can be perceived.

9

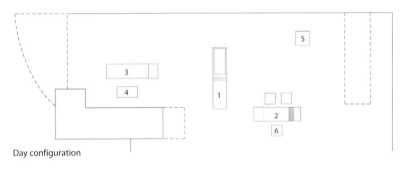

Day configuration

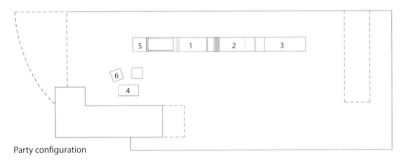

Party configuration

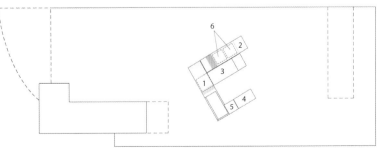

Night configuration

10

8 As much a showroom as a store, l.a.Eyeworks has always been keen to celebrate an alliance with creative fields.

9 The interior of the shop was designed to withstand changes in fashion and architectural style.

10 Moveable benches and shelving units allow various configurations for different uses.

1

The smart-travelling store is arguably what Berlin does best – an independent retail space that combines a quirky taste with a funky, individualistic sense of style. A new retail concept, the smart-travelling store was developed by Nicola Bramigk and her partner and designer, Werner Aisslenger. Inspired by her lust for travel, the store calls itself the first smart-travelling concept store, offering ultimate products for city travellers. Perhaps less of a shop than a travel-related experience, the establishment is housed in a long, 90-square-metre (969-square-foot), double-height space in one of Berlin's historic courtyards in the fashionable Mitte district.

An eclectic treasure trove, the shop sells, among other things, products from or relating to 19 European countries. Many of the items have been sourced by Bramigk on her trips or have been exclusively developed and produced by the smart-travelling brand. The items include travel guides and travel literature and gourmet food from around Europe, such as Austria's Marillenmarmelade and wines and oils from Italy.

2

1 The pink changing cube is to the left and the lamps-cum-clothes racks to the right. Electrical cables are buried under a layer of bark mulch underneath the clothes rails.

2 Simple timber shelving is used to display gifts and gourmet items from different European countries. Aquariums have been illuminated from behind to serve as display boxes.

In the front section of the store, the seven-metre (23-foot)-long fashion area features clothes racks that double up as lamps and a distinctive four-metre (13-foot)-high, freestanding unit made from the same fabric as the lampshades that also serves as a changing room and light box. The racks display clothing designed by Bramigk, with an emphasis on casual travelwear. At the other end of the space, two read/work lounges provide sofas and chairs where visitors can peruse the many books that are for sale. There is also a music station displaying CDs of music from around the world. The store also acts as the office headquarters for the travel services website. A screen set into the wall presents and explains the website and the store's concept.

Apart from the pink that is used in the lampshades and for the light box, the palette comprises neutral colours, with a polished concrete floor, oak shelves and white or black walls. Quirky touches, such as the pink light box, illuminated aquaria (sourced from a zoo), and a large map of Europe enliven the space. The central counter is also strikingly unique – a display cabinet from the 1950s that was bought on an auction website.

To keep it simple, spaces under the clothes racks are filled with bark mulch to cover the exposed electrical cables, done like this to avoid routing grooves in the walls for the cables. The overall design effect is one of sampling, where vintage pieces stand next to ingenious yet simple architectural interventions.

3

4

3 Vintage furniture sits among assorted items that are kept in the timber and glass display units.

4 The store's palette is neutral with a polished concrete floor and white or black walls. The sofas and chairs are provided as comfortable seating for browsing the books that are for sale.

5 Cheese, bread and a wall-mounted stag's head are just some of the items on display in one section.

6 At the end of the fashion area small, randomly placed shelves display a range of items from European cities.

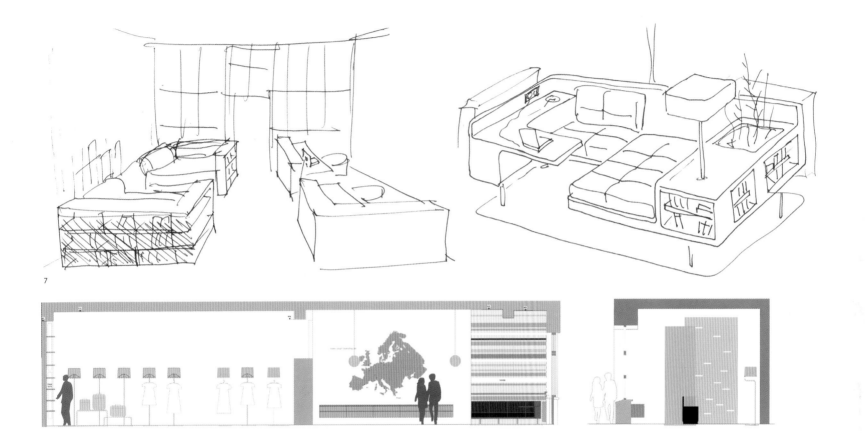

7

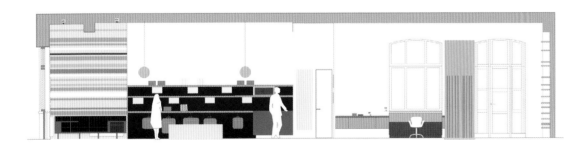

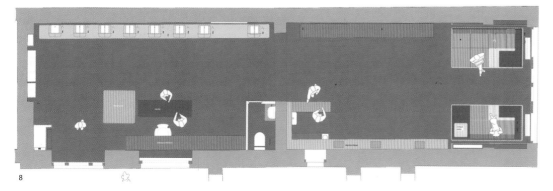

8

7 Sketches of the seating arrangements in the read/work lounge area.

8 Top and centre: internal elevations. Bottom: plan, with the lounge to the right and the fashion area to the left.

1

In 2004, in a conscious effort to fuse architectural cool and top-quality produce, Rocco Princi commissioned architect Claudio Silvestrin to create a 'boutique bakery' in the heart of Milan. Entrepeneur Rocco Princi is known locally for being the 'Armani' of bread, hence it was somehow fitting and ironic that he would work with the architect responsible for many of Armani's shops worldwide. Princi also owns four other bakery shops in Milan (the first opened in 1985) all specializing in local and international produce, with a strong focus on smart packaging and customer service via catering, bars and quick-snack food joints.

With Claudio Silvestrin's architecture, Princi wanted to emphasize the traditional, hand-made approach to baking and the quality of the produce. He came up with the idea of making the production visible to customers by moving the street-level kitchen to between the storefront windows and an internal glass wall. The fast-paced action of the 'laboratorio' is intended as a contrast to the calm of the store. Here the bakers knead over 200 types of bread, all visible to the customers and onlookers like a theatrical performance. Clad in chic Armani uniforms, the bakers are elegant and dramatic-looking.

Princi was also keen to employ constant reminders of the Italian artisan tradition. Thus the materials become a way of recalling ancient ways and places. Porphyry slabs of marble are the ones characteristically employed in the old town's *piazze* and historical centres, the laminated elements recall the workshops, while the wood tops are where one traditionally kneads the dough. The essential elements of fire, water, earth and air, each crucial to the art of breadmaking, are strongly present in the architecture as a fusion of an abstract sign and physicality of matter. Silvestrin chose an unusual mixture of colours: brass panels in a scorched-earth tone for the main desks and walls, slabs of smooth porphyry in a grey/violet tone for the floor and rough porphyry for the dwarf wall.

A parapet at the back of the store is a direct reference to Rome, set in a deep niche it houses a wood–burning fireplace. The parapet then turns into a long snack counter and then pierces the glass storefront where water trickles like a fountain from the wall. On the coffee counter, a Venini clear glass designed by Silvestrin is the lone decorative flourish. The seating is several Le Spighe bar stools, produced by Poltrona Frau and designed by Silvestrin, while the lighting is either discreetly set in the white ceiling or hidden in the ankle-level slits in the stairwell walls.

Silvestrin's signature purity and minimalism is, as forever, present – the 209-square-metre (2,250-square-foot), two-level space created for the Princi *panetteria* is stripped down to the bare essentials, so that the simple sensual pleasures of making bread can be fully indulged. The space is more gallery than retail, an oasis of calm and collected style, filled with delectable foodstuffs.

2

1 At the back of the store, set in a niche in a parapet, is a wood-burning fireplace.

2 Scorched-earth tones for the walls and desks recall one of the four essential elements.

3 The two-level space is stripped down to its bare essentials in Claudio Silvestrin's trademark, minimalist style.

4

4 Red stools by Poltrona Frau and designed by Claudio Silvestrin are used as seating at the long bar counter.

5 A staircase leads to the lower level, while lighting is hidden in slits in the walls.

5

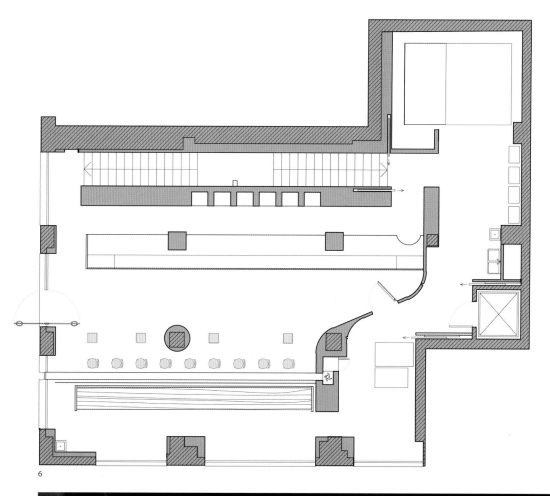

6

7

6 Plan: the entrance is to the left, staircase to the lower level at the top, and the laboratorio at the bottom.

7 In the laboratorio, well-visible to the customers, bakers knead and prepare over 200 types of bread.

1

1 A large metal theatrical mask and an optical pavement create a surreal space.

2 *Waiting for Godot*, by Samuel Beckett, is the text that has been used as decoration in the lower ground area and on the staircase.

3 Two large eyes made of tiles, one brown and one blue, dominate the showroom window.

Italian designer Fabio Novembre, known for his lavish and ornamental installations and love for tiles, was fittingly appointed art director at the German glass mosaic manufacturer, Bisazza, in 2000. Since then, he has designed Bisazza's showrooms in Milan, New York and Berlin. 'Tiles are always architectural elements for me. They are the skin of my spaces,' says Novembre, who likens his architecture to the 'body of a woman, sensual and full of curves'.

For the new showroom at Kantstrasse, Novembre devised a cornucopia of colours and shapes resembling a theatrical design – a theme already employed in the other Bisazza showrooms that also often hold performances and exhibitions. The inspiration for this showroom was Samuel Beckett's play *Waiting for Godot*. The reference to Godot is Novembre's interpretation of the city of Berlin, a metropolis that he believes has been constantly on the verge of 'becoming', and is the historic capital of 'suspense'.

Two large eyes, one brown and one blue, dominate the showrooms windows and attract the attention of passers-by. Made of glass tiles and displayed via a computer system, they are supposed to recall David Bowie's eyes – a man, according to Novembre, who does not wait for any Godot and represents the perfect example of creativity. The exotic, luscious interiors are tiled like canvases and carry many themes throughout the rooms: one has an optical style, another is more decadent in blues and gold, while yet another is decorated with Beckett's text. Downstairs, an all-white lounge with comfortable, white seats for reclining becomes a symbol for the eternal waiting.

2

3

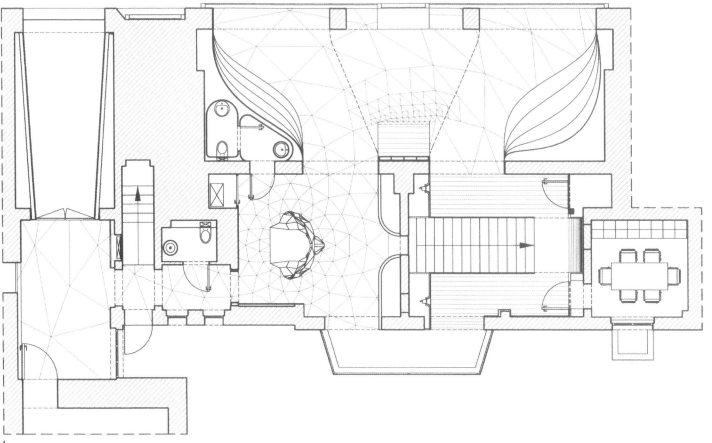

4

4 Plan: the upper level is dominated by the giant metallic mask (bottom centre)

5

6

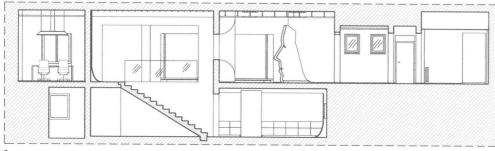
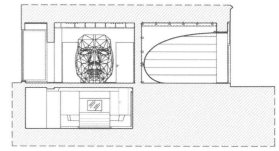

7

5 The staircase, decorated with Godot's text, leads to the downstairs area.

6 The exotic, luscious interiors are tiled like canvases and each room carries a different theme.

7 Long and short sections through the two-storey space.

After the success of her series of 'guerrilla stores' in 2004, Comme des Garçons founder Rei Kawakubo has created Dover Street Market in London's Mayfair. The total antithesis to most designer stores, it has been conceived as more of an artistic collective. The large shed houses the cash desk.

INTRODUCTION

The retail world has always flirted with art and now, led by the image-hungry, luxury end of fashion, art is finding in the retail environment an increasingly receptive outlet for exposure. At Dover Street Market in London, the boundaries between art space and retail floor space have been merged in a seamless mix of curation, sculpture and sales. Jenny Holzer's graphic installations have made an appearance at Helmut Lang (pages 170–173), while Issey Miyake's flagship store in New York (pages 178–181) now features the sculpted work of Frank Gehry. The lines between culture and commodity have been purposely blurred with a consumerist culture of shopping, elevated to the cultural high of the private view.

The art factor in retail is fast becoming an inspiration to shop interiors, producing sculptural forms and installation zones. As even the locations of art galleries (like SoHo in New York) become new territory for retail, shops mimic the art gallery's atmosphere, thus elevating the act of purchasing into a ritual. Hani Rashid of Asymptote looks at the similarities between retail and gallery.

INTERVIEW WITH HANI RASHID OF ASYMPTOTE, NEW YORK, USA

You have designed and built many different types of buildings. What are the main differences when approaching a retail commission?

'We approach all our work as projects about spatial issues – virtual or real, large or small. Essentially it's the same problem – how one perceives and comprehends geometry, enclosure, meaning and so on. What differentiates retail is that the space we design must have visual impact and provide a compelling backdrop to the retail experience. The problem with most retail design approaches is that they tend to privilege utility and "point of sale reasoning", which invariably leads to designs that make the experience predictable and mundane at best. In effect, shopping is not that far from experiencing any cultural phenomena in a controlled environment, such as art museums and galleries. The activity of looking at art has its parallel for us in retail design, since it's as much about the human spectacle as it is about buying.'

Today we see many 'types' of retail spaces, such as epicenters, shopping malls, boutique palazzos or simply low-key outlets that purposely eschew brand uniformity. Do you think any of these approaches are particularly relevant to today's culture or are they telling for our times?

'Yes, if our times are uninspired due to culturally levelled sets of experiences that make us all more or less the same across the globe. My optimistic hope is that we will find ways to bridge local and global concerns and effects, and perhaps some signals will emerge in the most public of spatial experiences – shopping. The central intention with the only retail venue we've realized this far was to place Carlos Miele, a Brazilian fashion designer, square in the heart of modernity and global flux, calling up though abstraction, art, and spatiality his cultural roots and inspirations while steering clear of Disneyland clichés.'

Shopping patterns have changed over the years and we have seen an increase in online purchase power as well as the consumer's backlash of the whole 'no logo' movement. In parallel, there is a whole spate of top-end fashion brands commissioning luxurious retail designs. As a designer, how do you create a space that people want to flock to?

'I am an architect who believes that people are drawn to elegance, excitement, enigma and beauty, no matter what the actual reason. A retail situation will obviously have a draw when it has things people want, and the question that prevails is always "What do people want"? As an architect involved in cultural building design, I have a conviction that people want environments that dignify them, and that is what any successful space does. The added value comes from supplementing that dignified condition with some mystery and unexpected spatial condition, something that causes a pause, thought or even inspires an intellectual experience, thereby speaking to peoples' need to feel something that's not only commerce-based, but also emotional and visceral. These real human needs will always transcend the solitude of the online experience or the shallowness of trends.'

Is shopping today more leisure or retail? What do you think contributes to creating an entertaining experience?

'The space between the somewhat highbrow experience of looking at art in the Chelsea neighborhood in Manhattan and shopping in SoHo is not that far apart. The same leisure/retail experience prevails and I find that fascinating – shopping for art or taking in the shop windows and brands are similar and intertwined activities. So the question as to what contributes to or heightens these experiences is an interesting one. Probably the answer lies somewhere between projection, fantasy and desire and flow, movement and ease of access.'

Many upscale boutiques use 'artistic devices' in their design. Is it an attempt to elevate the experience, a pretentious act or could shops really become the new gallery spaces?

'From my point of view we have not yet seen enough in this realm to really bring a level of profundity into the equation. At the moment there is far more lip service being given to such things rather than truly inspired experiences that hover between art and fashion, retail and gallery. So I fear that the sprinkling of art into these environments seems more pretentious and superficial than one would imagine it could be. We are seeing, however, more architectural consciousness in façades and materials, and that is probably because it's a safer, well-trodden terrain for brand management – less contentious.'

One could argue that other shops, such the experimental Prada Epicenter, use technology more as an art installation than a tool to make purchasing easier. Can it contribute to augment the shopping experience?

'Well, I wish I could say yes to either the art or purchasing aspects, yet the New York Prada store has failed miserably on that account – the over-inflated expenditures on interactive displays, electronically infused glass, computer- and web-aided interfaces, identity scanners, etc. This failure has unfortunately dealt a blow to more innovation in this realm, as the majority of these things are either not working, or not understood in their usage by customers and staff alike. Yet I do believe that, applied correctly, these technologies could serve as both an enhanced shopping experience and a more efficient and manageable situation for retailers. Unfortunately we have yet to see a seamless mesh of this capability in the retail environment in general, although one sector has been making considerable inroads in this domain, namely that of automotive purchasing, and perhaps that's where the best clues are. However, elevating these technologies to an art form and a truly inspired experience will still take some time. Prada was a noble attempt in the right direction, just not implemented correctly in my opinion.'

With its love of minimal, clean cut lines, Helmut Lang was always going to need an adequate retail space. The New York flagship opened in 1997 and spearheaded the whole trend of merging art with retail. In an attempt to challenge both traditional retail planning and the consumer experience, architect Richard Gluckman and clothing designer Helmut Lang renovated a 325-square-metre (3,500-square-foot) loft in SoHo, turning it into a space that mimics an art gallery. This retail strategy was expanded with Helmut Lang shops in Paris and Milan. The New York shop has obelisk-like light installations by Jenny Holzer and, in particular, the Paris one also contains works by Louise Bourgeois, with whom Helmut Lang has collaborated many times, and furniture pieces by Jean Prouvé.

The New York space consists of three distinct yet integrated parts. In contrast to traditional retail planning, the merchandising area is at the rear of the store, freeing the front for a reception area that is also visible from the street. A full-height, translucent glass wall draws the customer past the installation by artist by Jenny Holzer and into the main area. In the second of the three spaces, monolithic boxes, in rigorous succession, reveal themselves as freestanding cabinets containing the designer's collections. A long and low cash/wrap table runs parallel to the customer's path. The perimeter walls are not used for any display and act as a blank backdrop to the shop.

1

2

1 In this minimalist setting, the walls are not employed for display, but merely act as a blank back-drop to the shop.

2 One of the three monolithic black boxes that are actually freestanding cabinets containing the designer's collections.

3 Helmut Lang's store in SoHo clearly mimics the space of an art gallery.

3

4 Plan: the street façade is to the right and the retail and dressing area to the left.

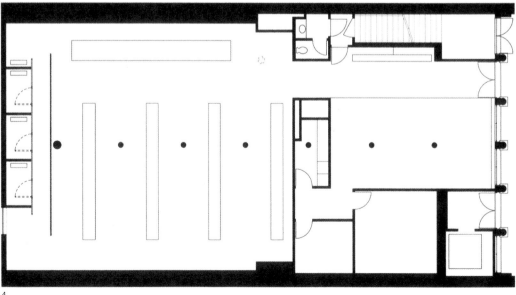

4

5

Concealed behind the translucent glass wall is the tall, narrow rear space that encloses the dressing room area and creates a private and elegant atmosphere. A continuous skylight above emphasizes the verticality of the space and a large window of blue glass provides views of the exterior space between the buildings behind the store.

Each of the three spaces is further defined by distinct lighting. The reception area is downlit by encapsulated PAR (Parabolic Aluminized Reflector) lamps, mounted in porcelain sockets; the merchandising area is uplit from the top of the cabinets by colour-corrected T8 fluorescent lamps; and the dressing rooms are exposed to natural daylight. The store stocks complete Helmut Lang collections, both for men and women, and a special service is provided, upon request, for VIPs.

6

7

5 The front area of the store is kept empty and used as a reception space.

6 Concealed behind the translucent glass wall is the tall, narrow rear space that encloses the dressing room area.

7 A few items of merchandise are displayed in minimal style on sculptural units.

In an attempt to reverse the now common association between fashion and high architecture, the Japanese Comme des Garçons founder and designer, Rei Kawakubo, opened a series of 'guerrilla stores' in 2004. These temporary flagships were built with very little money and in run-down spaces in unfashionable parts of towns such as Berlin, Singapore and Ljubljana. Understandably, the press was intrigued. This was, after all, the fashion visionary that had kick-started the whole retailer/architect love affair, most notably with the New York Comme des Garçons flagships store designed by Future Systems in the meat-packing district long before it become a location for retail flagships. Almost as a testament to the transient passing of fashion fads, the guerilla stores' life is one year only, after which it closes down.

The Dover Street Market is Kawakubo's latest retail venture, post the guerilla store concept. It is inspired by the energetic, collective anarchy of London's Kensington Market, which compressed the whole eclectic range of the London post-punk, independent designer scene under its one large roof. Dover Street Market is located in a Georgian-fronted property in Mayfair, not far from the chic retail heaven Old Bond Street. Yet Dover Street Market proposes itself as the very antithesis to the elegant, sleek, box format adopted by so many brands. Rather, it is conceived as an artistic collective where fashion, furniture, jewellery and theatre designers come together to realize a unique and eclectic vision.

Bare walls and naked steel beams define the store as anti-flagship par excellence, a concept that is entirely Kawakubo's. A backdrop of

1

1 The large shack-style shed, made of wood and laminated iron, houses the cash desk on the ground floor.

2 Dover Street Market's low-key façade purposely eschews the glitzy style of the more glamorous boutiques on nearby Old Bond Street.

3 Custom-made, low-cost timber display units, bare walls and naked steel beams define Dover Street Market's anti-flagship philosophy.

2

3

4

4 Murals and art pieces sit comfortably alongside vintage
furniture and fashion pieces.

5 Limited-edition collections are displayed on simple rail
racks while opulent chandeliers clash with the neon lights
in the office-style ceiling.

5

houses by the scenographer Elise Capdenat; Minotaurs by theatre designer Michael Howells were inspired by Kawakubo's brief 'Shakespeare meets Picasso'; murals on the walls; draped silk curtains; recycled taxidermy glass cases; a large 'shack shed' made of laminated iron housing the till… all reflect the industrial chic spirit as well as the low budget behind it. The fitting rooms are Portakabins, while collections are displayed behind metallic-bead curtains

The 1,208-square-metre (13,000-square-foot), six-floor shop is packed with freestanding art and fashion pieces, both vintage and bespoke. Jean Prouve chairs sit alongside a limited-edition furniture collection designed by Dior menswear designer Hedi Slimane. Rather than the representation of a single brand or value, it displays a community of designers, gathered together by the selective and discerning eye of Kawakubo. Beside the various Comme des Garçons ranges, Dover Street Market also displays Belgian menswear designer

Raf Simmons and his past collections; a boudoir boutique line by East London label Boudicca; hand-signed and hand-decorated Judy Blame jewellery pieces; Lanvin's designer, Alber Elbaz, garments; Fred Perry shirts; and box sets from photographer Nick Knight's archives. On the financial side, the company acts as a mall operator, taking a percentage of sales from each 'stall' to cover the costs of the 15-year lease.

In its bid to create an 'ongoing atmosphere of beautiful chaos' the Dover Street Market blurs the boundary between retail and installation art. Nothing is mass-consumed, nothing is readily available elsewhere, the focus is on the individuality of the purchasing experience.

French sibling designers Erwan and Ronan Bouroullec were approached in 2000 by Issey Miyake's team to design a space in Paris dedicated to his new clothes collection, APOC. For the Bouroullec brothers this was a first, since their background had been so far been in product and furniture design. Because the commissioner, Issey Miyake, was also a designer, the Bouroullec brothers found that they had to interpret their own brief-specific requirements from Miyake. These were limited to a bespoke cutting table and an ironing table that would evoke the idea of a tailor's workshop, where clothes are made to fit.

'APOC' is an innovative design concept by Miyake. It is made using an industrial knitting or weaving machine, which is programmed by a computer. This process creates continuous tubes of fabric, within which lie both shape and pattern. A thread goes into the machine and re-emerges as a piece of clothing or another shape – accessories or even a chair. The customer cuts sleeves and skirts exactly to the desired length, creating a totally customized final effect. The opposite of the current standard in clothes manufacturing, APOC proposes an interactive method in which customers have a say in the final shape of the product, while benefiting from a new technology. APOC merges the qualities of old-fashioned tailoring with mass production.

The Bouroullec brothers decided to conceive the shop as a playground for Issey Miyake and the APOC collection. 'We tried to design a shop that would be free from our own signature. Our idea was to consider that the experience of the customer would be defined by the clothes presented inside and the way they were arranged. The shop had to be incredibly minimal, but also totally disorganized and eclectic... We also specifically decided to use as little colour as possible, because we thought that the clothes would create a set of their own,' says Erwan Bouroullec.

The shop was designed as a changeable 'presentation tool': it can be full of clothes or alternatively show just one or two garments. Mirrors and tables can be changed around or removed. 'In a way we didn't impose any

1

1 The designers' original idea was to create a shop that would be a playground for Miyake and the APOC collection.

2

2 Most of the furniture is made of Corian, moulded to form continuously flowing, soft shapes.

3 Clothes are either fixed to the walls with magnets or displayed on hangers or rails.

3

4

4 A clothes line rail, made of Corian, allows the garments to be moved around.

5

5 Renderings of the interior, illustrating the curving display structures and hanging rails that surround the space.

6 The environment is kept minimal and with as little colour as possible to emphasize the clothes.

7 A green partition adds an unusual dash of colour to the store's environment.

6

presentation set, but opened some different, possible paths that the staff and Miyake could then follow on their own,' says Bouroullec. The interactive, changing environment reflects the nature of the APOC product, where customers participate in the creation of their own garments.

The design of the shop started with details such as the coat hanger, a support for the hanger and so on. There are dresses fixed to the wall with magnets, elastic fabric on rolls, stools for shoes and coloured markings for decoration and orientation. Most of the furniture is made of Corian: tabletops, display surfaces, hangers and 'assembly-line' rails that surround the space and allow 'pieces' to slide along. 'We used a lot of Corian, in a really "carved" way, which at that time was one of the most innovative uses for this material, especially in a large scale like a retail environment,' says Bouroullec. The Corian has been moulded to form continuously flowing, soft shapes. The cutting tables and ironing boards slip into tabletops and merge together without a visible seam. No hooks, no pegs, no strings can be seen because of the use of magnets. The 100-square-metre (1,076-square-foot) boutique is a totally white environment that works as a gallery, an atelier, a factory and a shop.

7

8

8 The modular style of the shop fittings reflects the nature of Miyake's APOC product, which can be customized according to the wearer's needs or likes.

Architecture takes on a sculptural function with Carlos Miele's New York flagship designed by Asymptote. The 325-square-meter (3,500-square-foot), single-level space is conceived as a sinuous and curvaceous environment, resplendent in high-gloss liquid finishes and textures. This is a prime example of the flirtation between fashion and art, which sees shops becomes increasingly more like galleries and often even competing for space in same areas of town. The Miele shop presents itself with a luminous façade that leads into a space bathed in a neutral palette of white and shades of pale green, green/blue and grey. The winding central space creates both a welcoming place for gathering as well as providing an ideal catwalk runaway for fashion events.

The design intends to celebrate Miele's perspective and aesthetic attitude towards design in his native country, Brazil. The design and architecture of the store embraces a culture that champions modern aesthetics while being steeped in traditional cultural rituals. The architectural environment becomes a spatial narrative, centred primarily on an abstracted reading of what constitutes Brazilian culture, landscape and architecture, while also being a contemporary experience of downtown, vibrant Manhattan life. The curvilinear forms are arguably an homage to the architecture of the legendary Oscar Niemeyer, and the contrast between technology and tradition reflects the different spirits of São Paulo (Miele's home town) and New York.

1

1 The designer's original concept was for a bright open space using a palette of white, pale green and grey. This was intended to serve as a backdrop for the brightly patterned cloths.

2 The high-gloss, epoxy flooring has embedded glass rings that are illuminated from underneath with neon and halogen lighting. Dresses are strategically suspended so that they appear to float over the rings.

3

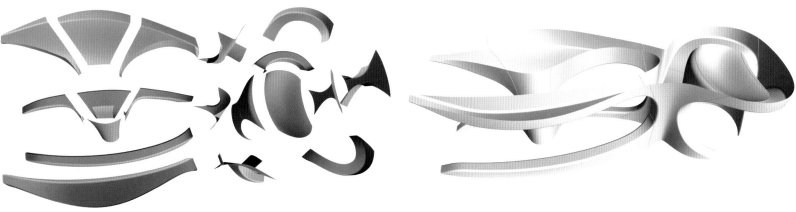

4

3 The central display structure was made from lacquered and bent plywood over a rib-and-gusset substructure.

4 From left: computer models of the display structure, in pieces and assembled.

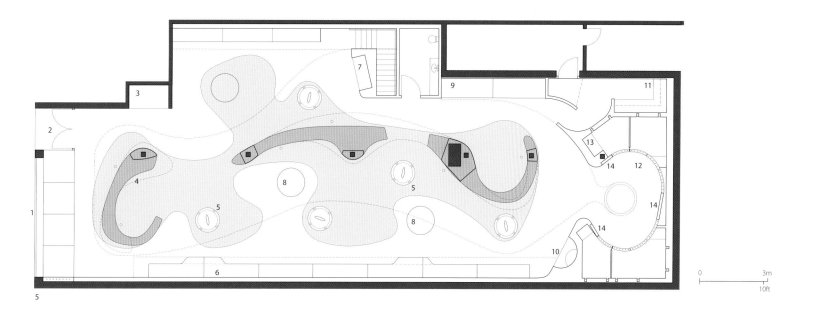

5

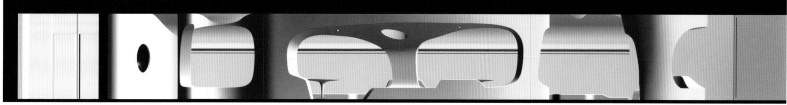

6

This contemporary setting of seemingly disparate, but not irreconcilable, opposite influences sets the stage for the presentation of Miele's brightly patterned clothes. The two-tone, shiny epoxy floor is divided by three sculptural partitions, whose form echoes the fluidity of the exposed clothes. The shape is the result of computer studies of fabric cuttings from the floor of Miele's design studio. A gleaming ceiling, made out of a high-gloss, stretched PVC-based material produced by Barrisol, further adds to the resplendent atmosphere of glossy whiteness. Mannequins float, suspended mid-air by wires. Their shining halos are the result of circular neon fixtures embedded in the floor to visually anchor the floating forms. Interspersed around each ring of light are MR16 lamps. A halo of light emanates overhead from a Par 30 individual fixture, to accent free-hanging mannequins.

The sophisticated environment also features digital art that has been integrated into the architecture in the form of two videos by Asymptote.

While one installation is encased in black, mirrored glass that reflects both viewer and merchandise, a second installation projects images of fire and water against a rear wall. Each piece celebrates an aspect of body and spatiality. These works are extensions of Asymptote's art projects, recently included in Documenta XI and the Venice Biennale.

'One should elevate an experience to the level of the art world,' says Hani Rashid. 'Designing galleries and museums has become somewhat an exhausted project, because the gallery can't seem to rise from the white-box syndrome…. For interesting architectural, spatial and artistic expression, the work has to be rooted in the everyday experience of the city.' With its high-tech organic shapes and cool and collected atmosphere, the Miele space perfectly frames fashion.

5 Plan: 1. West 14th Street, 2. entrance, 3. artwork niche, 4. 'altar', 5. light ring, 6. clothing, 7. display niche, 8. tables, 9. backlit clothing, 10. mirror sphere, 11. cashier, 12. changing area, 13. bench, 14. mirror.

6 Long section through two points in the store, with the entrance to the left.

PROJECT CREDITS

Issey Miyake APOC Store, Paris, France
Design Concept Erwan and Ronan Bouroullec
23 rue du Buisson Saint-Louis
75010 Paris, France
Website www.bouroullec.com
Client Issey Miyake

Alexander McQueen, New York, USA
Designer William Russell Architecture and Design Ltd, now
of Pentagram
Project Team William Russell, Michelle Hotchkin
11 Needham Road
London W11 2RP, UK
Website www.pentagram.co.uk
Client Alexander McQueen
Main Contractor Interior Construction Corporation
Architect of Record STUDIOS Architecture
Mechanical/Electrical/Plumbing MGJ & Associates
Hanging Metal Fixtures/Custom Millwork Mison
Concepts, Inc.
Terrazzo Floors D. Magnan & Co, Inc.

Apple Store, Tokyo, Japan
Architect Bohlin Cywinski Jackson
733 Allston Way
Berkeley, CA 94710, USA
Website www.bcj.com
Project Team Peter Q. Bohlin (design principal), Jon C.
Jackson (principal-in-charge), Karl Backus (principal, project
director), Anastasia Congdon (project manager), Joe
Holsen, David Murray, Mary Beth Coyne, Maria Danielides,
Rachel Lehn, Ben McDonald, Jennifer Rhoades, Lydia So,
Mike Waltner
Design Associate Gensler
Architect of Record/Engineer KAJIMA Design
Client Apple Computer, Inc.
Main Contractor KAJIMA Corporation
Structural Engineer Dewhurst MacFarlane & Partners, Inc.
MEP Engineer Flack & Kurtz, Inc.
Lighting Designer ISP Design

Maison Baccarat, Paris, France
Design Concept Philippe Starck
18/20 rue du Faubourg du Temple
75011 Paris, France
Website www.starck.com
Project Team Dorothée Boissier, Grégoire Maisondieu,
Astrid Courtois, Maud Bury
Project Architect José-Louis Albertini in collaboration with
Hervé Jaillet
Client Baccarat
Project Team Renaud Bereski, Emmanuel Cencig,
Alphonse Goberville, Christophe Schott, Claude Vizelle,
Jean-Claude Weinacker
Graphics Concept Thibaut Mathieu for Cake Design

Glass Blowers Michel Barge, Daniel Denain
Glass Manufacturer/moulder Serge Vanesson
Furniture Suppliers Atelier Thierry Goux, Droog Design,
Drucker, Emeco, ENP, Gaétan Lanzani, Ketta, Laval, Orssi
Engelo, Style et Confort, Techniques Transparents
Woodwork Siam Agencement
Mirrors Mirosyle SARL
Wallpaper Kvadrat, Lelièvrem Pierre Frey
Tapestries Plybe, Mallet
Floors SMD
Carpets Tisca, France
Luminous Carpets Fenaux Createx
Tablecloth in the Crystal Room Rorthault
Stucco L'Atelier Blanch'art
Decorative Paintings Gilles Plagnet
Bronzes Lambert
Sculptures Ion Condiescu
Video and Audio SES Giraudon
Lighting Concept Voyons Voir
Lighting Manufacturer L'Atelier Fechoz
Aquarium Coutant
Fireplaces Bloch

B&B Italia, London, UK
Architect John Pawson
Unit B, 70–78 York Way
London N1 9AG, UK
Website www.johnpawson.com
Collaborating Interior Designer Antonio Citterio with
Patricia Viel
Via Cerva 4
20122 Milan, Italy
Website www.antonio-citterio.it
Project Architect DCM – Denton Corker Marshall
Client B&B Italia
Client Manager David Zimber
Builder John Richards Shopfitters
Lighting Via Bizzuno, Flos

Bisazza, Berlin, Germany
Architect Fabio Novembre
Via Mecenate 76/3
Milan 20138, Italy
Website www.novembre.it
Project Team Giuseppina Flor, Ramon Karges, Carlo
Formisano, Lorenzo De Nicola
Client Bisazza s.p.a
Main Contractor Löhn Hochbau GmbH
Local Architect Arch. Carlo Lorenzo Ferrante – ION
Industrial Design, Berlin
Floorcovering Metron and Logos slabs by Bisazza
Wallcovering Vetricolor by Bisazza
Ceilings Barrisol Stretch lumiere ceiling
Windows, Glass Balustrades and Floor Glass Passage
ABC Gottschalk

Furniture 'Less' table by Molteni s.p.a., 'Aluminum Chair' by
ICF Company, custom-made furniture by F1
Lighting Modular Lighting Instruments, Erco, custom-
made lamps by Se'lux
Plasma Monitor LG Electronics

Bless, Berlin, Germany
Design concept Ines Kaag and Desiree Heiss
Mulackstrasse 38
10119 Berlin, Germany
Website www.bless-service.de
Client Bless Shop

Camper Store, Munich (and Barcelona)
Shop Concept Design Marti Guixé
Calabria 252
08029 Barcelona, Spain
Website www.guixe.com
Client Camper
Project Realization Camper Architecture Department
Lamps – Munich Ingo Maurer
Lamps – Barcelona Marti Guixé

Carlos Miele, New York, USA
Architect Asymptote
561 Broadway, Suite 5A
New York, NY 10012, USA
Website www.asymptote.net
Project Team Hani Rashid, Lise Anne Couture (principals),
Jill Leckner (project architect), Noburu Ota, John Cleater,
Peter Horner, Cathy Jones with Michael Levy Bajar,
Janghwan Cheon, Teresa Cheung, Mary Ellen Cooper,
Shinichiro Himematsu, Michael Huang, Lamia Jallad, AnaSa,
Marjus Schnierle, Yasmin Shahamiri
Client Carlos Miele
Main Contractor Vanguard Construction & Development
Engineers Kam Chiu, Andre Tomas Chaszar
Lighting Design Focus Lighting, Inc.
A/V Consultant Ben Greenfield
Fabricator 555 International

Christian Dior, Tokyo, Japan
Architect Kazuyo Sejima + Ryue Nishizawa/SANAA
7-A, 2-2-35
Higashi-Shinagawa
Shinagawa-ku, Tokyo 140-0002, Japan
Website www.sanaa.co.jp
Project Team Kazuyo Sejima, Ryue Nishizawa, Junya
Ishigami, Koichiro Tokimori, Yumiko Yamada, Yoshitaka
Tanase, Erika Hidaka
Interior Design Christian Dior Couture Architectural
Department
Client Christian Dior
Structural Engineers Sasaki Structural Consultants
Mechanical Engineers P.T. Morimura & Associates

Lighting Designer Kilt Planning
Builder Shimizu Corporation

Dover Street Market, London, UK
Overall Design and Concept Rei Kawakubo
Client Comme des Garçons
Drawings/Realization Ishimaru KK
Construction/Japan Ishimaru KK
Construction/England Mark, Richard, Steve at E.I.T.
Organization Adrian Joffe, Dickon Bowden
4th Floor and Basement Elise Capdenat, Theatre and
Dance Scenographer
1st Floor Michael Howells, film set designer, working on
the brief 'Shakespeare meets Picasso' given to him by Rei
Kawakubo
2nd Floor Jan de Cock, Artist
Ground Floor Reception Vedovamazzei Artists

Emporio Armani, Hong Kong
Architect Massimiliano and Doriana Fuksas/mFuksas Arch
Piazza del Monte di Pietà 30
00186 Rome, Italy
Website www.fuksas.it
Project Team Massimiliano and Doriana Fuksas, Davide
Stolfi (project leader), Iain Wadham, Defne Dilber, Motohiro
Takada (design team), Gianluca Brancaleone, Nicola Cabiati,
Andrea Marazzi (model makers)
Client Giorgio Armani
Floor Sikafloor
Furniture Massimiliano and Doriana Fuksas, manufactured
by Zeus Noto
Glass Showcase Sunglas
Lights iGuzzini
Vases in Armani Fiori Monte di Rovello
Façade Signage Nettuno Neon

Fendi, Paris, France
Architect Lazzarini Pickering Architects
Via Cola di Rienzo 28
Rome 00192, Italy
Project Team Claudio Lazzarini, Carl Pickering, Elisabetta
Biffi, Giuseppe Postet
Executive Architects Sopha Architects
Client Fendi, France
Project Management LVMH Fashion Group Real Estate
Department
Store Fitout Schmit Tradition
Quantity Surveyor Socotec
Services Engineer Espace Temps
Site Coordinator Methodes et Construction
Structural Calculation Staircase Bureau d'Etudes Lefevre

Gallery, Andorra
Architect Francesc Pons
Bonavista 6

Bajos 32
08012 Barcelona, Spain
Website www.estudifrancescpons.com
Client Robert Cassany and Sonia Yebra
Builder Pringeret
Metalworker Talleres fertin
Air Conditioning Trefelca
Carpenter Construmad
Pavement Gra Paviments

Globus Food Hall, Zurich, Switzerland
Architect Brunner Eisenhut Gisi Architects
Letzigraben 114
8047 Zurich, Switzerland
Website www.be-architekten.ch
Project Team ARGE, Eugen Eisenhut, Roger Brunner, Stefan
Gisi
Client Globus Zentralverwaltung
General Management Perolini Baumanagement AG

Gucci, New York, USA
Architect Studio Sofield, Inc. – Designers
380 Lafayette Street
New York, NY 10003, USA
Project Team William Sofield (principal), Emma O'Neill
(vice president), Douglas Gellenbeck (project manager),
Alberto Velez (senior designer)
Collaborators Brennan Beer Gorman (architectural
consultant), Gensler (architect)
Client Gucci Group
Lighting Consultant William Armstrong

Helmut Lang, New York, USA
Architect Gluckman Mayner Architects
250 Hudson Street
New York, NY 10013, USA
Website www.gluckmanmayner.net
Project Team Richard Gluckman (principal-in-charge),
Melissa Cicetti (project manager), Eric Change, Bobby Han,
Perry Whidden
Client Onward Kashiyama (Holding Company), Helmut
Lang
Consultants Ove Arup & Partners, Mechanical and
Structural Engineers
Main Contractors Eurostruct, Inc.
Glass Floral Glass
Cabinets American Woods and Veneers Work, Inc.
GFRC Essex Works

l.a. Eyeworks, Los Angeles, USA
Architect Neil M. Denari Architects, Inc.
12615 Washington Boulevard
Los Angeles, CA 90066, USA
Website www.nmda-inc.com
Project Team Neil M. Denari, Duks Koschitz with Carmen

Hammerer (publication graphics)
Client Gai Gherardi and Barbara McReynolds
Main Contractor Duran and Associates
Design Consultants Gordon Polon (structural engineer),
Julie Reeves of Lighting Design Alliance (lighting
consultants)
Specialized Surface Finishing Boxcar Studio
Mobile Furniture Fabrication K. B. Manufacturing
Fixed Furniture Fabrication John Ballesteros
Vacuum Formed Panel Art Installation Design Jim
Isermann
Custom LED Mandex Motion Displays

Liberty, London, UK
Architect 20/20
20–23 Mandela Street
London, NW1 0DU, UK
Project Team Rune Gustafson, formerly Managing Director
of 20/20 now Lippincott Mercer, Simon Stacey, formerly
Creative Director of 20/20 now of Lippincott Mercer, Sarah
Page (project leader – interiors), Sara Hilden (project leader
– graphics)
Client Liberty
Main Contractors AE Hadleys (shopfitting – cosmetics and
womenswear), JRS (shopfitting – menswear)
Consultants Davis Langdon (project management), INTO
Lighting (lighting designers)

Mandarina Duck, London, UK
Architect Marcel Wanders Studio
Jacob Catskade 25
1052 BT Amsterdam, The Netherlands
Website www.marcelwanders.com
Project Architect Harper Mackay
Client Mandarina Duck
Main Contractor Kingly
Lighting Consultant Modular Lighting
Mannequins, Gulliver free-standing mirrors The Set
Company
Glass Displays Studio LB
Floor Finishes Escopalatino, Desso
Wall Finishes Tyvek, DuPont
Multiple(x) Lighting Modular Lighting NL

Miss Sixty/Energie Emporium, Barcelona, Spain
Architects Studio 63 Architecture and Design
Piazza Santa Maria Sopr'arno 1
50124 Florence, Italy
Website www.studio63.it
Project Team Massimo Dei, Piero Angelo Orecchioni
Interior and Lighting Design Studio 63
Client Miss Sixty of Sixty Group
Furniture Manufactured by Buzzoni SRL
Lighting Manufactured by Nord Light

Mulberry, London, UK
Design Consultants Four IV Design Consultants Ltd
Exmouth House
3 Pine Street
London, EC1R OJH, UK
Website www.fouriv.com
Project Team Chris Dewar-Dixon, Richard Ryan, Louise
Barnard, Ruth Treacher (interiors), Kim Hartley, Paul Skerm,
Julie Austin (graphics)
Client Roger Saul, Godfrey David
Project Managers Mark Alford Associates
Main Contractor Bridport
Consultants EEP (mechanical and electrical), Campbell
(lighting), Michael Hadi Associates (structural engineers),
Kate Henderson (visual merchandising)

O₂, Munich, Germany
Architect, Interior Designer, Lead Agency, Multimedia
and Music concept Dan Pearlman Markenarchitektur
Kiefholzstrasse 1
12435 Berlin, Germany
Website www.danpearlman.com
Client O₂
Media Band ART+COM AG
Shopfitting/furniture Vizona GmbH
Lighting Ansorg GmbH

oki-ni, London, UK
Architect 6a Architects
6a Orde Hall Street
London WC1N 3JW, UK
Website www.6a.co.uk
Project Team Tom Emerson, Stephanie Macdonald
Client oki-ni (Paddy Meehan)
Main Contractor John Perkins Projects
Brand Consultant JJ Marshall Associates
Structural Engineer Jane Wernick Associates
Project Managers Dobson White Buolcott
Graphics Fuel

Orange, Birmingham, UK
Design Consultants Lippincott Mercer and 20/20
Address of Lippincott Mercer
1 Grosvenor Place, London SW1X 7HJ, UK
Website www.lippincottmercer.com
Address of 20/20
20-23 Mandela Street
London NW1 0DU, UK
Project Team Rune Gustafson, formerly Managing Director
of 20/20 now of Lippincott Mercer, Simon Stacey, formerly
Creative Director of 20/20 now of Lippincott Mercer), John
Regan (project leader – interiors), George Fountain –
project leader – graphics), Sarah Baboo – senior designer
(interiors)

Client Orange Retail UK
Main Contractor Bedford and Havehands (main
shopfitting contractors)
Lighting Designers INTO Lighting

Prada, Los Angeles, USA
Architects Office for Metropolitan Architecture (OMA-
AMO)
Heer Bokelweg 149
3032 AD Rotterdam, The Netherlands
Website www.oma.nl
Project Team Rem Koolhaas (partner-in-charge), Ole
Scheeren (partner-in-charge), Eric Change (project
architect), Jessica Rothschild (project architect), Amale
Andraos (project architect), Christian Bandi, Catarina Canas,
David Moore, Mark Watanabe, Torsten Schroeder, Joecelyn
Low, Keren Engelman, Ali Kops, Jeffrey Johnson
AMO Project Team Markus Schaefer, Clemens Weisshaar,
Reed Kram, Nicolas Firket, Michael Rock, Joakim Dahlqvist,
Stephen Wang, Richard Wang, Sung Kim, Dan Michaelson,
Leigh Devine
Executive Architect Brand+Allen Architects
Client Prada
Main Contractor Plant Construction
Structure Services Arup, Los Angeles
Lighting Kugler Tillotson Associates
Façade Skylight Dewhurst McFarlane
Curtain Inside Outside
Wallpaper and Graphics 2x4
Material Development Chris van Duijn (OMA), Werkplaats
De Rijk, Panelite, Plant Construction

Princi Bakery, Milan, Italy
Architect Claudio Silvestrin Architects
Unit 412 Kingswharf
302 Kingsland Road, London N8 4DS, UK
Website www.claudiosilvestrin.com
Project Team Claudio Silvestrin, Giuliana Salmaso
Client Rocco Rinci, Milan
Main Contractor BOMA
Structural Engineers Giulio Farina
Lighting Claudio Silvestrin in collaboration with
Viabizzuno
Air-conditioning Intesa Impianti
Interior Design Engineering Frontini & Battagin
Brass Covering in terra bruciata Silvestrin Astec
Stone Supplier Polimarmo

Pringle, London, UK
Architects Wells Mackereth Architects
Unit 14, Archer Street Studios
10–11 Archer Street
London W1D 7AZ, UK
Website www.wellsmackereth.com
Project Team Amy Lam, Sally Mackereth, Patricia

Miyamoto, Angelika Richter, Pascale Schulte, Yoko
Watanabe, James Wells
Client Pringle of Scotland
Main Contractor Pat Carter Contracts Ltd
Structural Engineer Whitby Bird
Mechanical Services Sidney Dubbage (H&V) Ltd
Electrical Services MCE Ltd

Selfridges, Birmingham, UK
Architect Future Systems
The Warehouse
20 Victoria Gardens
London W11 3PE, UK
Website www.future-systems.com
Project Team Soren Aagaard, Nerida Bergin, Sarah Jayne
Bowen, Lida Caharsouli, Julian Flannery, Harvinder Gabhari,
Dominic Harris, Nicola Hawkins, Matthew Heywood,
Candas Jennings, Jan Kaplicky, Amanda Levete, Iain
MacKay, Glenn Moorley, Andrea Morgante, Thorsten
Overberg, Angus Pond, Jessica Salt, Severin Soder
Main Contractor Laing O'Rourke
Structure, Services + façade Engineering Arup
Quantity Surveyor Boyden + Co.
Project Manager Faithful + Gould
Main Frame Contractor Sir Robert McAlpine
Glazing Subcontractor Haran Glass
Envelope Subcontractor 5M
Disc Manufacture James +Taylor
Stainless Steel Panelling Subcontractor Baris/Jordan
Sprayed Concrete Subcontractor Shotcrete
GRP.GRG Subcontractor Diespeker
M&E Contractor Haden Young

Shoebaloo, Amsterdam, The Netherlands
Architect Meyer en Van Schooten Architecten BV
Pilotenstraat 35
1059 CH Amsterdam, The Netherlands
Website www.meyer-vanschooten.nl
Project Team Koert Göschel, Oliver Oechsle
Client Shoebaloo BV
Main Contractor GF Deko
Furniture Normania
Installation Lighting Philips Nederland BV
Glazed Entrance Glaverned
Polyester Furniture Meyer en Van Schooten (design),
Normania (manufacturer)
Glass wall covering Altuglas by Atoglas
Glass Floor manufactured by Saint Roch
Curved glass skirting board Tetterode Glas
Lighting Manufacturer Philips Nederland BV

smart-travelling store, Berlin, Germany
Design Concept Werner Aisslinger with Nicola Bramigk
Studio Aisslinger
Oranienplatz 4

10999 Berlin, Germany
Website www.aisslinger.de
Project Team Werner Aisslinger, Thom Spycher, Tina
Bunyaprasit, Fred Fréty, Manuel Vital, Till Grosch, Bao-Nghi
Droste
Client Nicola Bramigk
Furniture Design Werner Aisslinger

Stella McCartney Store, New York, USA
Architect Universal Design Studio
35 Charlotte Road
London EC2A 3PG, UK
Website www.universaldesignstudio.com
Client Stella McCartney
Main Contractor Interior Construction Corporation
Lighting Design Campbell Lighting Design
Millwork/Specialist Joinery Cappellini Contracts
Tile Designed by Barber & Osgerby, manufactured by
Teamwork Italia

TOD's, Tokyo, Japan
Architect Toyo Ito & Associates, Architects
1-19-4 Shibuya
Shibuya-ku
150-0002 Tokyo, Japan
Website www.toyo-ito.co.jp
Project Team Toyo Ito, Takeo Hisashi, Akihisa Hirata, Kaori
Shikichi, Leo Yokota, Takuji Aoshima, Yasuaki Mizunuma
Client Holpaf B.V.
Main Contractor Takenaka Corporation
Structural Engineers Structural Design Office OAK, Inc.
Mechanical Engineers ES Associates
Furniture Design Toyo Ito & Associates, Architects
Fixtures and Fittings Design Modar srl, Garde U.S.P Co.,
Ltd.

Villamoda, Kuwait City, Kuwait
**Architects, Concept, Lighting Design, Co-ordination
of Interior Design** pfcarchitects
Via Giangiacome Mora 7
20123 Milan, Italy
Website www.pfcarchitects.com
Project Team Pierfrancesco Cravel
Collaborators
Eldrige & Smerin Architects (interior design of multibrand
areas, external landscaping, restaurant/café, lounge and
public areas)
Client Green Cedars spa
Main Contractor Al Ahlia Contracting Group
Engineering Favero & Milan Ingegneria
Building Management Gulf Consult Kuwait
Brand/identity Designers Wink Media (now Winkreative)
Furniture Suppliers Coexistence, SCP, Cappellini

Y's, Tokyo, Japan
Principal Designer Ron Arad, Ron Arad Associates
62 Chalk Farm Road
London NW1 8AN, UK
Website www.ronarad.com
Project Team Ron Arad, Asa Bruno (project architect),
James Foster (architectural assistant), Paul Gibbons (3D
visualizations)
Executive/collaborating Architect (Japan) Shiro Nakata,
Studio Mebius
Client Yohji Yamamoto
Client Representative Mr Fujio Hasumi
Main Contractor Mr Minoru Kawamura, Build Co. Japan
Specialist Subcontractor (loops) Mr Roberto Travaglia,
Marzorati-Ronchetti
Lighting Consultant iGuzzini

INDEX

PHOTO CREDITS

The publisher would like to thank the following sources for permission to reproduce images in this book:

Soren Aagaard (78 bottom, 79, 80 bottom), Peter Aaron/ESTO (18–20), Sue Barr/VIEW (10 right), Courtesy Bless (102–103), Luc Boegly/artedia (2, 142–147), Nicola Bramigk (155, 156 left), Richard Bryant/ARCAID (6 left, 7 left, 7 right), Benny Chan/Fotoworks (148–153), Courtesy Comme des Garçons (166–167, 174–177), Courtesy Colette (9 right), Courtesy Conran & Partners (10 left, 11 left), Richard Davies (7 second from left), diephotodesigner.de (122–125), Alberto Ferrero (162–165), Floto + Warner (34–35, 41 left, 42–43), Klaus Frahm/artur (8 right), Dennis Gilbert/VIEW (9 middle), Richard Glover/VIEW (130–131, 138–141), Lydia Gould (38–40, 41 right), David Grandorge (44–47), Courtesy Gucci (6 middle), Roland Halbe/artur (10 middle, 11 right), Ken Hayden (6 right), Heinrich Helfenstein (134–136), Stefan Jaenicke (154, 156 right), Nick Kane/Arcaid (78 top, 80 top), Christoph Kicherer (7 second from right), Inga Knölke (100–101), Morgane Le Gall (174–175, 177), Eric Laignel (60–63), Dieter Leistner/artur (13 right), André Lichtenberg (96–97, 110–112), Aka Son Lindman (92–95), Peter Lippsmeier/artur (13 left), Fredrika Lökholm (11 middle, 12 left), Jeroen Musch (48–51), Nacasa & Partners (52–54, 86 right–91), Tomio Ohashi (86 left), Koji Okumura (114–115, 126–128), Frank Oudeman (82–85), Keith Parry (14–15, 30–33), Andrew Peppard (26–29), Matteo Piazza (72–75, 158–161), Yael Pincus (106–109), Eugeni Pons (76–77), Prat Ramon (64–67), Jörg Schöner/artur (9 left), Shinkenchika-sha (68–71), Edmund Sumner (56–57), Kenichi Suzuki (8 left), Paul Warchol (170–173, 178–180), Adrian Wilson (22–25, 118–121), Łucja Zielińska (12 right)

Author's acknowledgements

A special thanks to all the designers and architects who submitted material for this book. In particular, I would like to thank Rune Gustafson at Lippincott Mercer for his invaluable insight on retail, Neil Churcher for his knowledge of technology and interaction design, Terence Conran, Amanda Levete at Future Systems, Sally Mackereth at Wells Mackereth, everybody at Dan Pearlman, Hani Rashid, Marcel Wanders and Markus Schaefer for taking time to address the different issues explored in this book. Finally, I would like to thank everybody at Laurence King Publishing for making the project possible, especially Jennifer Hudson for all the research.